In My Brothers Footsteps, The Battle Back

A True Life Story of Triumph over Tragedy

Allan Rykoff

authorHOUSE®

AuthorHouse™
1663 Liberty Drive, Suite 200
Bloomington, IN 47403
www.authorhouse.com
Phone: 1-800-839-8640

First published by AuthorHouse 4/20/2009

ISBN: 978-1-4389-4301-5 (sc)

Printed in the United States of America
Bloomington, Indiana

This book is printed on acid-free paper.

INTRODUCTION

<u>In My Brothers Footsteps, The Battle Back</u> is a poignant, heart- warm-
ing and sometimes funny accounting of my life. It tells of love, trust, fear,
dismay and conquest. From a little boy with ADD, learning life's lessons
the hard way on the streets of New York, to a misguided troubled youth,
to growing up in the prison system and then founding one of the most
successful drug treatment programs for youth in the country.

The story centers around my relationship with my older brother (by
six years) who led me down the road of drugs, crime, and prison until
I fought back with the help of a therapeutic community to become the
person I am today. The book also serves as a reminder for parents and
teachers of kids with ADD and /or drug-related problems that something
must be done immediately.

The problems of ADD and drug abuse are devastating and, if not
dealt with, can lead you through a lifetime of anguish and I know that
the more we tell parents and teachers about these concerns, the easier it
will be for them to recognize and deal with them.

This book was written the way I speak, from the heart with the flavor
of the streets in every word.

This is my story, I hope you enjoy it.

CHAPTER ONE

My story begins in Brooklyn, N.Y., on the borderline of Brownsville and East Flatbush, a pleasant, middle-class Jewish community. The year is 1939. There were four of us in the family, my mother, father, an older brother by six years and me, the baby of the family. This was a great area to be raised in. The buildings were mostly four family houses with some apartment houses thrown in. Each house had a little garden with a tree in front of it. The neighbors all knew each another and were friendly, always stopping to talk or helping each other. On sunny weekends, all the people were in front of the houses talking, smiling and laughing. It took forever to walk up the block. "Hi, Allan, how's your mother?" "O.K. How are you?" "Hello, Mrs. Berman, how are you?" "Hi, Mrs. Schwartz. How's Mr. Schwartz?" "Fine Allan, How are you?" This would continue on from building to building, it was like one big happy family.

Milk, seltzer and syrup were delivered to your door. You were also able to shop by phone and it would be delivered to your house. I remember that well because I was the kid making the deliveries on a bicycle when I was about twelve and thirteen years old. I always worked at that age, going from store to store asking for jobs, and worked for many of those stores in those days, not at once, but over time I worked in a lot of them.

In those days, there were no supermarkets. Instead, there were stores that sold meat, others fish and seafood, and others sold fruits and vegetables; and, of course, there were grocery stores and candy stores. The stores were all lined up. In my area, they were all located on East 98th Street with a few others scattered throughout the area.

On my corner there was a triangle separating Lennox Road from Kings Highway. There we had a candy store, a grocery store, a Chinese hand laundry, a T.V. repair shop and a barbershop. The barber's name was Charlie. Everyone in the area used Charlie the barber including my father, my brother and me. I remember that when my father was sick, Charlie would come to the house and give my dad a haircut and a shave, always trying to help out. People were like that then, always respecting and helping one another. Your storekeepers were your friends. Everyone was treated with respect.

Child abuse was not heard of in those days. Your parents, uncles, neighbors, storekeepers, schoolteachers, priests and rabbis would never harm a child. It was a time of good morals and values. This was a great time to grow up, and a great area to be brought up in.

Sports was the topic of conversation and all the neighbors would sit and watch the baseball games in the schoolyard, always routing for their neighbor's kid. "Go ahead; knock one out of the park" they would yell when you came to the plate. Then there was stickball, punch-ball, stoopball, triangle and johnny-on-the-pony. These were games that most kids today never heard of, but they were good games and we played our hearts out. We were all sport fans at that time. It was always the New York Yankees against the Brooklyn Dodgers. I was a Brooklyn Dodgers fan, my brother was a New York Yankees fan and my mother was always happy when the World Series was over because the wars between us would end.

Every Sunday, we would jump on the bus and go to see Grandma and Grandpa on Alabama Ave. in the East New York section of Brooklyn. I liked the bus ride there with its wide windows. I would always sit and watch people walking and talking, trying to figure out what they were thinking. I used to think that I could tell what type of person they were by the way they dressed, walked and acted. I'll never know if I was right or wrong, but it was fun thinking I could.

My grandparents lived in a four-family house at 651 Alabama Ave, 2nd floor, in the front of the building. The neighbors in the rear apartment were Lou and Vicki, who owned the candy store on the corner. To us, they were like family, always in and out of my grandparents' house. They also came to every family function we had. They were great people. I used to love going to the candy store that Lou and Vicki owned and I would always order a frappe. A frappe is what they call a sundae today. You had your choices of ice cream loaded with fresh walnuts and syrup, topped off with whipped cream. Lou knew just how I liked it, with plenty of nuts and syrup and loads of whipped cream. They would always say, "Here, Allan, special for you because we love you." Well, I loved them also.

All my aunts and uncles would be there with my cousins. We never missed a Sunday at my grandparents' house. My mother had six siblings and they were all married, with two children each, and my grandparents would pack all of us in the house. My family was very close and there was lots of love between everyone.

Once we got off the bus, it was a two-block walk to the house, and the anticipation of seeing everyone was great. I would always try to walk fast, but my mother would say, "Walk with me, Allan." As we opened the downstairs door, you got a whiff of the aroma from Grandma's cooking. It filled the hallway and you couldn't wait till she served.

When you opened grandma's door there were so many people that the hellos would take forever. Each aunt and uncle wanted a hug and a kiss. And grandpa, God bless him. When he hugged you, you knew you were hugged. He would hug you for a few minutes rubbing your cheek next to his, give you a kiss and tell you how much he loves you. Grandpa was a sports fan and loved kids. He would always umpire the baseball games in the neighborhood and all the kids in the area knew him as Grandpa Friedkin (his last name).

Grandma was a cripple who had one leg shorter than the other and one shoe had this large heel. She was the nicest, sweetest lady you could ever meet. With her nice Jewish accent she would always say "Allan, have more." The accent always sounded like she was saying "Ellen," not "Allan." I don't know what it sounded like to my cousin Ellen, but some day I must ask her. We always ate together, the entire family. After lunch, all the kids would go downstairs and play. "Look out for one another," we were told each time we left the house. As I got older, I made lots of friends on that block, and even played on a football team made up of guys in my grandparents' area. I loved going there every Sunday, looking forward to it each week.

I remember my grandfather taking me for walks. He would always take me to Linden Blvd. to a farm that milked cows. We would be on the second floor looking down at the cows that were hooked up to these machines for milking, and the cows would be rotating in a circle. Very slowly they would rotate and I enjoyed watching that, trying to figure out if I could pick out the same cow twice by its markings.

I also remember my uncles taking me for a ride to get their car washed. We would sit in the car while it went through the car wash. I also remember the owner of the car wash would always walk over and hand me a driver's license. On it, it read "back seat driver's license." When we returned to my grandparents' house, I would always run to my mother and show her, "Look ma, I got a driver's license." I was so proud of my driver's license.

We also had a family society named after its founder, Nachama Naischuler, my great-grandmother. It was called the Naischuler Family Society, made up of the entire clan, first cousins, second cousins, and the entire family. There were a few hundred people that used to meet every month at the Broadway Central Hotel, located in lower Manhattan. There was a board of directors meeting held each month to discuss family business. After the meeting was over, it became a social gathering. Each member would pay dues and the money would go for the care of the cemetery where the family would be placed once they were deceased. The family plot has stone benches with the names of deceased family members engraved, walkways and a large stone entrance. The money would also go for a vacation. Each summer, the whole family would rent the entire hotel, the Singer Hotel, which was located in New Jersey, and enjoy a couple of weeks together. This is, and still remains, a very tight knit family. I remember going to the monthly meetings when I was very young and enjoying seeing all the relatives. The only thing I didn't like was when my mother would say "Come here, Allan, let me wipe all the lipstick off your face." Damn, didn't women blot their lips in those days? The family society meetings still continue to this day and it has to been 88 years since it started.

I remember the block parties on every block the day we learned that World War II was over. We celebrated at my grandparents' house. They had two sons and a son-in-law in the armed forces. My uncle Sammy, a decorated war hero in the army, along with my dear uncle Sid, married to my aunt Bobbie and my famed uncle Bernie, in the Coast Guard. Bernie being Schoolboy Bernie Friedkin, a great featherweight and lightweight fighter during the late 30's and early 40's, and one of the nicest people you can ever meet. Bernie was loved by all who knew him. He was the only other family member we had in Brooklyn, and he would come over every once in a while to play ball with me and my friends. He tried like hell to help my mother and myself, always giving of his time and advice.

My childhood started off great, always playing, smiling and laughing. At five years old, like all other children, I started kindergarten. Believe it or not, I still remember some things from my kindergarten days. I remember bringing my pet turtle in to race with another kid's turtle and I remember playing musical chairs and yes, of course, I remember sitting in those small chairs in a semi-circle listening to the teacher talk.

My father and I had a great relationship. He was a milkman working for the Borden Company. At that time, he had a horse and wagon. The horse, a tall grey horse, was named Patty. Dad used to pass by and take me and my friends for a ride down the block in the horse-drawn cart. He would always leave us at the corner so we didn't have to cross the street to get home. My dad always kept me safe and I always felt very secure around him.

I remember watching the snow come down. I would sit by the window for hours just watching it snow and I knew that as soon as it stopped, I'd be sleigh riding down the hill behind the synagogue at the corner. To this day, I still think it's beautiful when the snow is falling. I would be at the window in the living room watching the snow for hours and my father would call me to the kitchen, give me some cookies and I'd go running back to the living room to look out the window again. He seemed to know when I finished my cookies because just then he was calling me back for more. I remember once my mother wanting to put me to bed and I was hiding from her because I wanted to stay up a little longer. My dad would tell me where to hide, and when mom would ask my dad if he saw me, he would say, "No."

My mother and my father had a great relationship. Dad, the milk-man, and my grandfather, a carpenter, used to eat lunch at the same res-taurant every day and got very friendly. They were from the same town in Russia and although they didn't know each other in the old country, they always shared stories of the old days. My father was planning a trip back to the old country to visit his family and my grandfather asked that he take pictures and letters back to share with my grandparents' family. My father did and, upon his return, had pictures, letters and stories to tell my grandfather. They were in the restaurant and my grandfather told my father to forget about telling him everything. "Come to dinner tonight, meet my family and tell us all."

My father did and that's when he met my mother. It was instant love. My father asked my mother out on a date and she said "Yes." In those days, you went out for months before you even held hands but my father knew what he wanted and asked my mother to marry him on the first date. It took my mother three months to say "Yes." They married in December, 1932. In the Jewish religion, you can't get married with a yellow gold ring; it has to be white gold. Later, my father bought a yellow gold ring for my mother but she refused to take the white ring off. Today, I wear that ring on my pinky and refuse to take it off.

A week after the marriage, they had an argument and my father raised his voice. My mother told him, "If you ever raise your voice to me again, this marriage is over and you will never see me again." He never did raise his voice again. After that, they had only two disagreements, one of which was about the color of the paint for a room they were painting, the other I'm not sure of. They got along just fine and loved each other very much.

Things seemed great then, and I was a happy kid; but there were some problems that I was unaware of. My dad was dying of cancer. I did not know how sick my dad was but I do remember as a kid when the fathers played punch-ball against the kids in the backyard my dad only played once. It had been a while since the fathers started playing against the kids but my dad, because of his illness, never played until one day my father walked into the backyard and said, "You guys got a spot for me?" I looked at him and said, "You playing, dad?" and he said, "Yes, son." I was so happy and I remember turning to my friends and saying, "Hey, my dad is playing," and as I turned back I could see Mr. Schwartz, my neighbor, smiling at my dad. Dad hit a ball to me. I think he wanted me to make a good play but I dropped it on purpose and my dad was safe at first base. We both looked at each other and I think we both knew what was going on. He wanted me to look good and I wanted him to be safe on first base.

A few months later while I was in kindergarten, my father passed away. I was five and a half, my brother was eleven and mom was in her mid- 30's. I remember walking into my house and my mother was in the bedroom crying. As I walked into the room, my mother grabbed me by the shoulders and started screaming, "Daddy is dead, daddy is dead." I also remember my aunt Roz telling my mother not to do this to me. I didn't understand death at this time. I left the house and walked across the street where my friends were sitting on the stoop and I said, "My father is dead," and my friend Henry started to laugh. I still didn't understand and my friend Arnie said, "You going to let him laugh because your father is dead?" and then I started to fight with Henry but in my head I had no idea what was going on or why I was even fighting. Nobody ever told me about death or what dying was all about. I didn't know and I had no idea that I would never see my dad again. The most tragic part is that when my father died, the entire family died. The family structure was gone and my mother wasn't strong enough to hold the family together. Soon I learned what death was about and soon I realized that dad was never coming back home. It was a sad time for the entire family and to my mother as I look back now, life had ended for her also. My brother and I were feeling so terrible and very depressed, hurt and lost. All three of us were. Dad had held the family together. He was the cornerstone. He and my mother had a great relationship. They had thirteen years of a great marriage. My mother would cry his name at night and that never ended till the day she died at eighty-one years old. Every once in a while, I would hear her at night in her sleep. She just never got over my dad's death. None of us ever did.

Shortly thereafter, I was in first grade. I had what's known as ADD. At that time, school officials didn't know what this problem was. I just couldn't pay attention and all I would do was sit and twirl my hair with my finger and look out the window. School was going on but I was some place in space. Whatever the teacher was talking about just went in one ear and out the other. After months of not paying attention and not doing my homework, I was labeled a bad kid. Reality is, I didn't pay attention because I couldn't pay attention. I sat in class not listening and I knew at that time I couldn't follow the teachings and school, as it was, is a waste of time for me. In those days there were no diagnoses and no medications for my problem, and nobody even knew I had a problem except me. I'm six years old and unable to figure it out or communicate it to the proper people so I soon became the bad boy in school, the kid that didn't pay attention and teachers would always ask me to sit in the last row, in the last seat. In every class I was in the last row, last seat. The fact was, I wasn't a bad kid, I was a good kid that was treated like the bad kid because of my problem and because nobody understood that I had a problem.

As the year changed and I entered the second grade, I went right to my seat and my reputation preceded me. Teachers knew that was my seat. I soon started to feel so different, like I didn't belong. All the kids were into education except me, and I started to feel like the outsider looking in at something that was foreign to me. That's when I started to think, "Why me?" "Why me?" "What's so different about me?" A terrible and disabling feeling came over me. Why was I so different from the rest? Why wasn't I like all the others who smiled and enjoyed learning, like those that were learning? Soon I figured, if I'm the bad kid, then let me act the way they wanted me to act, "like the bad kid." I soon became the bully in school, always fighting, grabbing girls by the hair, knocking books out of kids' hands, pushing and fighting with whoever I wanted and I was always getting into trouble. Because I couldn't pay attention, I also felt stupid. What a feeling it is to believe you are stupid, that you don't measure up, that you're not as good as the next person. You try not to think about it and find other ways to compensate but that doesn't work either and you become different than the rest. I was always failing my tests or passed on the borderline of failing. The funny thing was, I had a very high I.Q. but was unable to channel that to my schoolwork.

My problem was compounded by my older brother who was much smarter and sharper than I was. Any time I did something wrong, which was almost every day, I was called stupid. "You're stupid," he would yell. Well, call a person stupid enough times and, compound it with low scores in school, and you begin to believe you're stupid. I continued on in school always getting into fights and not listening to my teachers. When an argument started, I didn't have the word power to defend myself or present my case. It became very frustrating to me. I was so frustrated that one day I swung at someone and had a fight. I soon learned that I was good with my hands and this became the way I defended myself from verbal attacks, by fighting. If anyone said something I didn't like or hurt my feelings, I would lash out. I continued on like that through elementary school. Now by the age of 11, I was still not able to pay attention and I was stupid along with being heavy. For that my brother was calling me "Hippo." To him, it was a joke. To me, it was tragic.

Needless to say, I wasn't feeling very good about myself. I was stupid, fat, not as good as the rest, and I was a bad kid as well. I remember once at the age of 12, I asked my mother why she had me. I was a very unhappy child in a world of my own and not able to understand why, who or what but, to people in school, I was just a bad kid. I was also battling depression. I used to wish I was dead. Life meant nothing to me at that time. I didn't care about anything or anybody for that matter. I was loyal to my family and my religion because that's the way you were supposed to be but there really wasn't much love in my heart. Once my father was taken away from me by death, I became afraid to love. I had lost the person I loved most in this world and it hurt so much. I did love my mother but the ones I loved most in this world were my brother and my grandparents. For those people I never lost any love. To say I was depressed would be an understatement.

When we were very young, my mom worked in the house making wigs for a guy named Abe who lived on my grandparents' block. Abe was a nice guy with a hunchback who knew the family well. I remember Abe coming to the house to deliver hair and my mother, who was at my grandparents' house, had called. I answered the phone and she asked to speak with Abe. They spoke for a few minutes and then Abe said, "Come with me, Allan. Your mother wants me to take you to your grandparents' house." We got into Abe's car and he started to drive. When we were waiting for the light at the corner of Hegeman and Rockaway Avenues, Abe was saying, "You know, Allan, grandpa has been very sick lately." "I know Abe, I know that," I said. Abe replied, "Well, Allan, grandpa will never be sick again," and I knew my grandfather was dead. Not another word was said. Tears were rolling down my eyes but I just kept looking out the window and didn't say anything, not a word.

I got to the house, ran upstairs two steps at a time, got to the door and the entire family was there and I was told grandpa has died of a heart attack. I was crushed. This time I understood death. This time I knew I'd never see my grandfather again and I loved my grandfather so much. He and my brother had equal billing in my heart. The whole family was touched by grandpa's passing, not only the family but also the entire neighborhood. Grandpa was known to all around the area for a few reasons. Because, as I said, he was Grandpa Friedkin, the umpire of baseball games, and because he was the father of the great boxer Schoolboy Bernie Friedkin.

Grandma left the house only once after he died. I remember it was a Sunday afternoon and she was sitting in front of the house on a bench very quietly. Like my mother, her life ended when grandpa died. The nice sweet lady died six years later almost to the day my grandfather died. I loved them both and I miss them very much. Morris and Bessie Friedkin were two beautiful people.

My brother started acting out when he was young. At age 15, he had already been in youth house three times. He never wanted me to get into trouble so he used to tell me, "If you go to youth house, they tie you up and beat you." This was his type of therapy. I guess he figured I'd be scared and not get into trouble.

Soon I found myself in junior high school, Somers Junior High School, located right across the street from my house at 373 East 95th St. There, my reputation went along with me and again I was in the last row, last seat and now I was acting out even more. I was older, bigger and stronger with superior upper body strength. I don't remember a day going by that I wasn't in a fight or some sort of trouble. I remember one teacher, my Spanish teacher, telling me, "Allan, sit in the last row, last seat, don't say a word and I'll pass you." This, on the first day of the new school year. Hey, to me, this was great. I could slide by without being noticed and when I got to her class I sat in my seat and didn't say a word. I passed Spanish. "Hola."

In other classes I acted out, though. I guess sitting quietly for 40 minutes in Spanish class made me even crazier and once I left that class, I went looking for trouble so much that I became very destructive to the school and my 8th grade class was in the Assistant Principal's office. Yes, I would sit in Mr. Young's office all day long. I did that for about two months and then I told him, "This is getting us nowhere. Why don't you give me two classes of wood-working a day and two classes of gym a day?" He did just that.

In the morning, I would go to wood-working class and, in the afternoon, go to the gym. They weren't trying to help me; they were trying to keep me quiet. They were sacrificing one kid for the sake of others. Education, as we know it, was gone. In reality, I never had a chance at education since my first days in school. Some days I never even showed up and nobody knew I was gone. I had figured out that wood-working and gym aren't home class, so no attendance was taken. As far as those two teachers were concerned, I could have been any place, in the principal's office, in a classroom that taught a subject, any place. They didn't know and they didn't care.

I became a loser so early in life. I was supposed to lose, I thought. I wasn't as good as the rest. I remember once entering in a 40-yard dash in the 6th grade. (P.S. 219) The whistle blew starting the race and I got off the line so fast and was in the lead. I couldn't believe I was leading. I didn't belong here. My friend Arnie was coming up on my left and I knew I could kick. I knew I could speed up and win this race but I just let Arnie win because I didn't believe I was supposed to win. I was the loser. That's the way the teachers saw it and that's the way I saw it.

I'm pleased to say that after 52 years of not seeing one another, Arnie and I were reunited and stay in contact by phone and emails and we look forward to seeing each other again real soon. Maybe some day, we can do the race again; only at our age, it would have to be a three-yard dash. "I love ya, pal."

I remember my sixth grade class was giving a play at the end of the year. "Ali-Baba and the Forty Thieves" was the name of the play. The teacher was doing auditions for the lead role and I was called to talk. As I spoke, one girl said, "He's got the right voice for the part," and the teacher said, "Yes, but not the emotions." I thought about saying, "You didn't ask for emotions, I'll give you emotions," but I knew she didn't want me for the part and I just let it go. She was testing voices but that was her excuse for not picking me for the lead. She thought I would forget my lines or screw something up. As the play went on, I was saying the lines to myself, before the lead player said them, to see if I really could remember them. I remembered every word of every line. I knew just where the lead player was supposed to be on stage at each moment and I could have given a great performance but I was the loser and wasn't supposed to get parts like that. My problem was books. I was never able to comprehend what I'm reading but if you have my attention and tell me something or show me something, I never forget it.

I always did seem to get what I wanted no matter what I had to do, legal or illegal. One time, I saw this beautiful bicycle in the schoolyard not chained up. I stole it and cycled right to the police station, brought the bike in and said to one of the officers, "This bike has been in the schoolyard for two days so before someone steals it, I thought I'd bring it to you." "What a nice thing you did, son. If nobody claims it in ninety days, it's yours," said the officer. I replied, "Really? That would be great." I gave them my name and address and left. I had known the law before I did this and I knew that if I ride the bike around my house I would be caught so I turned it in hoping nobody would claim it. I had forgotten all about it and one day I walked into my house and saw this beautiful bike standing there. My mother told me that the police called and said that nobody claimed the bike, "So I called Uncle Bernie and he picked it up for you. It was all rusty from being in the warehouse but I cleaned it up for you. Allan, that was a good thing you did." When my mother said that, I felt guilty but I had my bike and that's what counted to me at the time. I was about twelve years old then and already manipulating the system.

In my 13th year of life in 1953, I brought a gun to school. I may have been the first kid ever to do that but mine, thank God, was a Red Ryder B.B. gun. I was outside of the school shooting up the windows, lights and whatever else I could see. The school administration called the police and later that day, as I was walking home, I saw Mr. Young outside the school talking to the police. He walked away after pointing me out to the police and they called me over. "You have a B.B. gun?" they asked. "Yeah," I said. They asked me, "Where is it?" "In my house," I said. "Let's go and get it," the policemen said. We went into the house and I couldn't remember where it was because I had hid it from my mother and forgot where I put it. I was also very nervous. We were in the bedroom and one officer was getting mad that I wouldn't produce the gun and pushed me onto the bed and there was the gun under my blanket. They took the gun and at the tender age of thirteen I was arrested, written up and sent home.

A few days later, my mother received a letter telling her to bring me to the police station. She did. We took the bus and went to the precinct on Empire Blvd. We sat in front of an office for 45 minutes and I was getting restless. I just couldn't sit any more so I got up, left the police station, got on the bus and headed home. A few weeks later, I got a letter to come to children's court in downtown Brooklyn. I went to court twice and each time the case was postponed. On the third try, my mother woke me up in the morning and said, "Let's get ready for court," and I said, "Mom, I'm not going. If I go today, I will be sent away." She tried to console me. "No," she said. "They're not going to put you away." I knew they were. I felt it, so she headed out the door by herself and off to court by herself. A few hours later, a court clerk called me and said, "You better get down here right away," and I told him, "No." I didn't like authority figures. I had no respect for authority. At the same time, I just knew I was going to be sent away and I was so frightened, so scared. I wanted no part of the youth house. I wasn't going to put myself in a position to be tied up and beaten. I just was petrified. I kept pacing around the house, thinking, where could I go, what could I do, how could I get away from this? There was nothing I was able to do. I couldn't think of a single thing, any way to get out of this situation. There were no answers. I wracked my brain and came up with nothing. There's got to be a way to get out of this, think, think, but there was nothing. If I stayed around the house, the police would pick me up. Where would I go, what could I do? There were no answers. My brother was serving a three-year sentence upstate New York and he could not help me. My friends were in school and they could not help. I was alone and felt that way. I was trapped.

Shortly thereafter, my aunt Roz was calling. She said "Allan, I'm going to pick you up and take you to court," and I remember thinking, "What can I do? Where can I go? I'm 13 years old without any money," so I said, "Yeah, come on over." I knew then I had lost again, I was defeated. She came and we went driving down to the courthouse.

I was nervous, very nervous, and my mom suggested that I go to the corner and buy gum to chew so I walked into the hall and started down the stairs when the court clerk stopped me and asked where I was going. I told him that I'm going to the corner for some gum and he said, "No, I can't let you go. You escaped from the police station." "Escaped," I thought. "I walked out the front door. This is what they call an escape" and I walked away chuckling to myself. The court clerk turned his back and down the stairs I ran. I went to the corner, bought some gum from the nice old blind guy that had this paper stand and walked back to court holding up the gum to show him he was wrong. I sat with my mother and my aunt and I was wishing I were someplace else, any place else, but not here in this courthouse.

I thought about what I had done with my B.B. gun but dismissed it from my mind knowing it was too late now to think about that. What I was thinking about was youth house and the beatings. "No, they're not beating me," I thought. "I'll fight back; I'll do anything but let them beat me. If they try and beat me they must kill me because I'm not taking it, I'm not going to let them beat me." The more I thought, the more the fear entered my head. I need a miracle, I thought, just one miracle God, that's all, just one.

My case was called and I walked in with my mother and my aunt. The judge was speaking but it was over my head. I didn't understand half of what she was saying. I did hear that the judge was going to send me to Kings County Hospital for observation. She said that I would be there from this date to that date and for some reason now I didn't believe it. I was so afraid to go to court knowing I would be sent away and now that I heard it from the judge, I didn't believe it or maybe for fear, not wanting to believe it. The mind can play some very strange games at times. I heard my mother crying in the back of the court and now it seemed like I was being sent away. I wanted to turn to my mother but I just knew I would start to cry also, so I kept staring at the judge. Right at her eyes, I kept staring and she said, "Walk over there." Well, over there was a desk and I thought I have to sign some papers and go two or three times a week. That's O.K. I hope that's all it is but as I turned, this big guy took me by the arm and walked me upstairs and now I knew I had pushed too hard and now I knew I was being locked up. What a feeling walking up those steps knowing that now the game was over, now there was no place to run and now I couldn't escape if I wanted to. As I walked up the stairs, I could still hear my mother crying and pictured my aunt holding her, but there was no one to hold me. I was alone entering a new phase in my life that was unknown to me and I was so scared.

The court clerk in charge of the prisoners, for lack of a better word, was Tony, a tall guy about 6 feet tall and pretty well-built. At the top of the stairs was a large room with other kids my age and a little older. Some were sitting at tables and some were standing. I really wanted to cry but my image got in the way. How could I cry in front of all these other guys, when my brother is in and out of jail and he doesn't cry? I looked to the ceiling in an effort to have the tears roll back in my eyes. That trick really doesn't work. Soon I gathered myself and started talking to the guys. Everyone there was headed for youth house. I knew what awaited them. That's where they tie you up and beat you. I was safe. I'm going to the hospital.

About an hour or two later, the bus came and they called all the names for youth house. I was hoping my name wasn't on this list and I was listening intently. My name was the last to be called. I walked over to Tony and said, "Hey, what's going on? You know I'm supposed to go to the hospital. Why you taking me to a youth house?" He said, "No, don't worry, kid. You're just going for the ride, and then we're coming back here to wait for an ambulance." I said, "That's OK. I don't have to take the ride. I'll wait right here for you." He said, "I can't let you do that, you escaped from the police station." "Again with the escape," I thought. "I didn't escape," I said. "I walked out the front door." I had always looked at escapes as going over the wall or digging under it. I guess I watched too many movies. In reality, I was right, but couldn't put the thoughts together. There was no escape. There was no intent to escape. I wasn't being held for anything. I had an appointment with a detective and I left before I saw him. That's it, but escape, that's out of the question.

Still so frightened, reluctantly I entered the bus. In the bus were about six or eight girls going to girls youth house, then an empty row of seats, and then the boys. When we arrived at the boys youth house, Tony announced, "All the guys get off the bus." All the guys got up and walked off the bus. I stayed in my seat. "Come on, Allan, let's go," said Tony. I said, "I'll wait for you here." I was told that the bus has to drop the girls off at the girls youth house then come back for me. "O.K." I said. "That's all right. I'll take the ride with the girls." He just would not let me do that so here I was on the ground floor of a youth house where they tie you up and beat you and I was so scared. I had been fighting and losing every battle all day and now I'm going to be tied up and beat. "This can't be," I said to myself. "This just can't be. How can they defy an order from the judge? This isn't right. It's not fair," I thought. After a few minutes they started to call the names of everyone going upstairs and, of course, my name was last on the list. I saw a water fountain and asked the counselor if I could get a drink. I was stalling for time. I figured even 10 seconds less up there is better than going right up. I drank so much water that soon the water was just going in my mouth and coming right out and the counselors told me to "stop stalling and come on now." With this, I panicked and ran across the room and grabbed Tony by his shirt. "You son-of-a-bitch," I screamed. "When I get out of here, I'm going to kick your ass." "What's the matter?" He asked and I told him, "You know I'm supposed to go to Kings County Hospital and you got me locked up in this f--king place." "Oh, no, he's coming with me," he told the counselor. Finally, finally, I won one and I was so relieved.

Soon the bus returned and we went back to the courthouse, back up stairs and waited for an ambulance to pick me up. At this point I was drained. Too many emotions in one day, too many battles for one day and I knew then, this time I'm going to escape for real. I just had to find a way. I just had to get away from what now was the most dramatic day in my life. They call me an escapist. I'll soon show them what escape is all about.The ambulance arrived and we walked downstairs. I looked around, "Can't make a move here," I thought. We were in a screened enclosure. Tony opened the door to the ambulance and we both got in. I couldn't see out the window but I knew when we were on Kings County property. Kings County Hospital is like a city with twisting, turning roads and so many buildings. Tony doesn't know it but he's got problems with me. I'm getting the hell out of here. I tried in my head to follow the route of the ambulance but there were just too many turns so I decided that when the door opens I'm darting out of there and heading for the nearest gate. I knew the hospital and I knew the gates were taller than I but I was going to follow the gate till I saw an opening.

The ambulance stopped and the door opened, but there was big Tony right at the door and I could not do a thing. He walked me inside holding my arm and I knew I had to switch plans. We walked down a long corridor with very high ceilings and hanging lights to an opening with several offices in a circle; then the corridor went out the other end. I sat in an office next to a desk, turning my head to look down the hall and out the door. Tony was out of sight. Finally, he was gone. In walked a doctor and a nurse's aide, along with about five or six candy stripers wanting to see this crazy kid get interviewed. I didn't like that; it really got me even more pissed. It was bad enough that I was here but now I'm on display for all these girls to watch this crazy kid get interviewed. As the doctor was talking to me, I was looking down the hall. It was time to make a move but just then some guy walks by lighting a cigar. "That jerk," I thought, "Get moving." Now I'm being asked about drug use, about the troubles that I have and I just can't take any more. Just then, as I'm ready to dart again, some guy walks by reading a newspaper. "Damn, I need a clear path. I'm going to make it, I'm going to make it," I thought. Now I'm crazed. I'm running out of time. I've got to make a move before they take me upstairs. Again the questions are coming and this time I jump off my chair, the nurse's aide reaches for me and I backhand him and go running out the door. Well, I got one foot out the door and there was Tony on the other side of the wall. He grabbed me by the shirt, lifted me up and put me back into the room. The emotion in that room at that time was scary. Tony was mad, the nurse's aide I hit was mad, the candy stripers were frightened and huddled in a corner, the doctor was nervous and I was so pissed that my plan had failed.

The doctor tells the nurse's aide to take me upstairs. "Hurry, get him upstairs," he says. We get in the elevator. He's not talking to me and I'm not talking to him, emotions are high. Thoughts are going through my mind, "What's next? It's him and me and he's a very big guy but I'm not backing down." We get off on the second floor and walk to this big metal door with a thin glass about four inches wide, almost the width of the door, and I said to myself, "Damn, they got me in a dungeon." With a long skeleton key, he opened the door and we walked down a long corridor with offices on both sides to another door with the same description. As he opened that door and I walked into the room, I was amazed at what I saw. There was rock and roll music playing, boys and girls were dancing and I remember saying, "What the hell is going on here? Is this a party?"

The nurse's aide walked me across the room to another door with the same description and he opened it. In front of me was a nurse's station with long corridors on both sides in a V shape. I was told to walk down to the fourth door on the right and wait in the room for him. As I walked down the hall, I knew something was up. "Why didn't he take me into the office? Isn't there paperwork to be filled out? Shouldn't I sign some papers?" I thought. The corridor was well-lit with bedrooms on both sides. I was scared. It was a moment of truth.

I walked to the fourth room on the right and it was a bathroom. I now knew what was coming, just what I had been expecting. I walked in, walked to the window and put my foot up on the radiator and was looking out the window. The room was large with about four or five toilet stalls, a few urinals and sinks and some showers. I stood at the window, just staring out. I stood there for about ten minutes just staring out the window, wondering what's going to happen once this guy gets to the bathroom. I was scared, but calm in my actions. Soon I heard footsteps, someone coming. "It's him," I thought. In walks the nurse's aide. A tall husky fellow, he stood there like the jolly green giant. Legs spread apart, arms folded and we both stared at each other. Our eyes locked on each other's for a few minutes. Nobody moving, nobody talking, eyes just staring. There was no way I was going to let this guy beat me. If he wanted war, war is what he's going to get. After a few minutes of this staring, he reached in his pocket, pulled out a pack of cigarettes and said, "Want one kid?" "No, I have my own," I replied. This nurse's aide liked me and, to be honest, I was more than relieved. He thought I had a lot of nerve and he saw no fear in me. Yes, I was scared, very scared, but with all the emotions of the day I was also crazed and ready for action. Anything at that time would have set me off.

We talked for a few minutes and I started to relax and calm down. Then he took me around and introduced me to all the older guys. They housed kids up to 16 years old. I was thirteen. After about an hour the older guys asked if he could put me in their room and move this guy they didn't like out. He did and now I was in with the good boys. Good boys meaning the tough crowd, the gang, the in-crowd.

I remember my first night there. They took us up to the third floor to watch a movie. After the movie had ended, we were in the hall waiting for the elevator to take us back down to the second floor. I was talking to this kid Rocco. Rocco was a nice kid, but while talking to him he started to slide down the wall that he was leaning up against. I remember saying, "What are you doing Rocco? Stop f--king around." Rocco hit the floor and started shaking. The nurse's aide ran over and stuck that big skeleton key in his mouth. Rocco was an epileptic and was having a seizure. That scared me and I kept away from Rocco as much as I could after that. That too created a problem because Rocco liked me and wanted to be my friend. He would follow me all over the place. Rocco didn't have many friends. I guess his condition scared more than just me. I just could not get rid of this kid and one day Rocco and I had a fight. We were down at the end of the hallway fighting. Within seconds here came the cavalry: two nurses' aides running down the hall. They broke up the fight and took me into the office. Thank God it was Nurse Johnson who was talking to me because she was a good lady. "Allan, don't you know Rocco can die fighting like that? What started the fight anyway?" she asked. So I told her and she explained that Rocco doesn't have many friends here and it would be nice if I was his friend. After that, I gave Rocco enough attention so that he wasn't always on my back. To Rocco I say, "Sorry, pal. If you're still out there, I wish you the best."

Being in with the older guys was challenging. True, I was accepted into the group with open arms, but because of my age, I wasn't going to let them think of me as the kid. I had seen that too much with my brother and his friends so I had to find some way to become the leader and I did. First, the day I got there, the nurse's aide told the guys what happened downstairs in the office, that I tried to escape. The guys liked that. They knew I wasn't afraid to fight because they saw the fight with Rocco and I always was a schemer. I came up with all the ideas. Each night we had to turn in our pants and shoes and they would put them in a closet till the next morning. Hell, I wasn't going to walk around the hall in my underwear and no shoes so I figured out that I could put them in my locker and turn my locker around to face the wall. My friends followed suit.

I remember my friend and another kid fighting it out down the end of the hallway. "Kick his ass," I was saying to encourage my friend. "Kick his ass." Then I looked up and saw some nurse's aides running down the hall. I stepped in between the two fighters and said, "Break it up fellas, someone's going to get hurt." The nurse's aide told me that I did a good thing. "No problem, sir, just doing the right thing," I said to the nurse's aide. The nurses' aide told me, "Don't worry, I'm going to put this in your folder. You're looking good, kid." The guys thought that was smart of me since the fight was going to be broken up anyway.

One night, two of my roommates were planning to go into another kid's room during the night and force this kid to perform oral sex on them. They asked me to join them. "No, not me," was my reply. Now they knew

I wasn't a follower. I felt sorry for this kid who they were planning on attacking, so a few minutes later I walked into the room in an effort to stop the rape only to find out there was no attack. The kid was gay and enjoying it more than they were so I walked back to my room and went to sleep. "Not my business," I thought.

A few days later, my mother came to visit and brought a care package made up of a home-cooked meal, candy and a carton of cigarettes. Inside the bag were about 10 books of matches which we weren't allowed to have. Remember, we were there for observation. When you wanted to light a cigarette, we had to ask some nurse's aide for a light. This we didn't like because at night when we were supposed to be in our rooms sleeping, we wanted to be in the bathroom smoking. I told my mother she wasn't allowed to give me matches and I stuck my hand in the bag pulling out all but four packs of matches and handed them to my mother. After mom left, I walked into the nurse's station and saw Mrs. Johnson. I told her that my mother made a mistake and left two books of matches in the bag. She came up to me and said, "Oh, great, Allan, I'm putting this on your chart." I was looking good again and still had two books of matches for myself and my friends. To my friends, I was now bringing in contraband. Becoming the leader wasn't hard; it was rather simple because I was a good schemer.

Every couple of days we would see the psychiatrist in those offices between the two metal doors. It seemed so easy to manipulate them as well, to tell them what they wanted to hear. The doctor asked me how I was feeling. I told the doctor, "I'm doing just fine, doc. What a fool I was to do what I did. Gee, I could have really hurt someone. A good thing I didn't, I would have felt terrible." "As easy as pie," I thought, and I was now manipulating the system once again.

It turned out to be not such a bad place. There was a gymnasium, which I loved. I had plenty of friends and the girls would come over just about every day from the girl's ward to dance. The staff was great, especially Mrs. Johnson and the guy I called the Jolly Green Giant because I can't remember his name. He and I became friends and used to speak a lot. He always tried to give me good advice. These people were so nice that, after my release, I went back a few times to visit.

On the day of my release, I had to go back to court and face the judge again. After three weeks in the Kings County Hospital mental ward for observation, the diagnosis that was read to the judge said I was emotionally upset and would outgrow it. Outgrow it? You will soon hear what happened in the years before I outgrew it. I was then placed on probation and sent home with my mother.

I now became the hero of the gang, the first one to enter the court system and be put away. Yes, I was the hero, but my friends didn't know the fear I had gone through, they didn't know how I looked at the ceiling trying to get the tears to roll back in my eyes, they didn't know how I felt walking into youth house thinking I was staying there. They only knew one thing. "Al went through the court system and was sent away." I was the hero, the first one of my crowd to go through this.

A few days later, I was called to see a social worker and he said, "Well, son, you have to go back to school.""I'm never going back to school," I said. The social worker replied, "O.K. then. Let me make it legal for you." I was assigned a private tutor. Just that simple. One sentence from me and two from him but those three sentences made things so much worse in my life. Now I was thirteen years old and legally out of school. I don't know what would have happened had I gone back to school. I don't know if I would have conformed to the system or if I would have gotten into more trouble, but you certainly don't take a kid out of school and make it legal for him because he says he's not going back. You may put him in the same school or send him to another school but you just don't take him out of school. The tutor came twice, once to tell me what type of books to get, and the second time she came, I screamed at her to get the hell out of my house. I wanted no part of her and no part of tutoring and no part of school. The poor lady got so scared she ran out the door and never returned. My mother was beside herself, but my concern was getting rid of this lady and anything to do with schoolwork. I never heard a word about it from the social worker, the probation department or the school board. Again, the system had failed me.

But let me stop for a while and bring my brother into the story. Stan didn't have my problem in school. My brother was one of the smarter kids going through the educational system at that time but he, too, had an acting-out disorder. At the age of 13, he broke away from the good kids he hung around with, and started to hang out with the gangs and the kids stealing cars. He was a very negative person and almost everything he did was against the law. Stealing whatever he could, smoking pot and only God knows what else. My brother at that time was my role model. He used to walk me to school and pick me up again when school was over until I was old enough to go and come by myself. As we got older, mom was out working at the Gund Manufacturing Company running the office there to support us, and my brother was just about raising me and we were each getting in trouble in our own way. He had started using drugs at a very young age. First, he started to smoke pot; then he started to use hard drugs. Heroin was the drug of choice then. I saw him and his friends using drugs in my house just about every day. I got really involved in the drug culture, although I still wasn't using. I had always thought drug addicts were crazy. I used to see them come into my house. Once in a while, they would be sick from not having any drugs and they would be sweating and talking about how cold they are. They would be throwing up and running to the bathroom every few minutes with diarrhea. "This is crazy," I thought. "These guys are nuts. What the hell do they do this for?"

One day I remember my brother waking me in the middle of the night. He said, "Come sleep with me in my bed. I just saw daddy." "Are you crazy? Daddy is dead," I said. "No, no, I saw him," he said. He had really gone off the deep end, I thought. Well, at age thirteen, if your older brother tells you to do something, you do it. We walked to his room and I got in his bed and as soon as he fell asleep, I got up to go back to my room. I walked out of his bedroom and made a right turn to walk through the kitchen and standing right in front of me was my father's ghost. He was on the other side of the room. From the waist up, there was my father, a white image looking at me. I got scared and turned on the light which was right next to me on the wall and the image was gone. To this day, I still wish I hadn't turned the light on and always wished he would come back. I should have tried to talk to him, to find some way to communicate, but I was young and afraid and reached for the light. I would expect that he came back trying to give my brother a message that obviously my brother never got. That time my brother was right, my father was there. There isn't a person on this earth that can convince me that there isn't some sort of life after death. I saw it myself, with my own eyes.

When I was 13, my brother, who was 19, was selling drugs out of the house. I had seen it a thousand times, my brother selling to his friends. I started to learn that business so well that when he wasn't home and a customer would be at the door, I serviced them. I would then give my brother the money and he would always hand me a few bucks. Yes, at age 13, I was selling drugs, hard drugs, heroin. It had become a way of life, nothing out of the ordinary, just routine. He needed the drugs sold and I liked money. The two went hand in hand.

Soon after, my brother started getting put away for longer periods of time. When he was 16, he got three years at the New Hampton Farms Reformatory in Middletown, New York, for stealing a car. My way of thinking had become so warped, for this and for all the other negative things he did, he was my hero and I wanted to be just like him. I saw him manipulate people so easily. I saw him with the toughest guys in the neighborhood and they would bow down to his brain. He was the leader, the mastermind. He was the guy I wanted to be. Oddly enough, our lives became so much alike. He was the first of his friends to be put away and I was the first of my friends to be put away. He was in a youth house at thirteen; I was in Kings County Hospital at thirteen. He went to the New Hampton Farms Reformatory and I did also, only now it was on Rikers Island. He had a ripped tendon in his left pinky and so do I. We were mirrors of each other.

We also looked so much alike that at 16 years old I was driving with his driver's license that had his picture on it. We sounded so much alike that when my mother would call on the telephone she never knew who she was talking to. We would tell her if it's Al or Stan. Once I remember needing some money to get high with and wanting to call my mother, but mom always refused me, although she never refused my brother, so I called her office. "Ma, this is Stan. I have to borrow 20 dollars." "O.K." she answered. "Come to my office." "I'm going to send Allan," I said. "O.K." she answered. When I got to her office, I told her Stan sent me to pick up 20 dollars and she gave it to me. That's how much we sounded alike that my own mother couldn't tell us apart. It wasn't right what I did and I knew it then but I was an addict who needed money and one does whatever one could to get it, although I will say proudly that I never stole any money or anything from a relative or a friend. Sometimes people in the streets would make a mistake. "Hey, Stan, how are you?" they would say to me, and I would always laugh. "You blind," I would tell them, "I'm the better-looking one." We looked alike, talked alike and started to think alike and I couldn't have been happier.

While my brother was in Raymond Street Jail awaiting a sentence for a crime he committed, I was bringing him drugs on the visit. I was about 15 years old but lied about my age to get in. Once, while putting the heroin in a cigarette that the tobacco was removed from, I had some left over and tried it. You know the saying, "Try it, you'll like it" and that was true in this case. The feeling of the high itself can't be described. There isn't an addict or an ex-addict in the world that can describe the feeling of a heroin high, other than to say it's a good feeling. In reality, it gets you to forget who you are inside. Most addicts are hiding from themselves and this drug is the mask that hides you from yourself. That night, I fell asleep with the television on and the ashtray on my stomach. In the morning when I woke up, my mother said, "What happened to you last night? When I walked into the room, the television was on and the ashtray was on your stomach." I hadn't moved a muscle all night. "I don't know, ma. I was really tired last night," I told my mother.

I now was stealing cars and fighting a lot and running in packs. Although I was running with this crazy crowd, I never lost my zest for baseball. During the summer months, I would always play baseball. That started with the less than 5-foot team while I was still in school. We used to get measured up against a wall and I remember always making myself limp in an effort to shrink a little. We had a good team and would play every day during the summer. Later, my friends and I started a team called the Cobras and we belonged to a league that was run by a sporting goods store in the area. If your team won, you came in for a new bat or a baseball. Each week, we would walk in and claim our prize. That was softball and I played either third base or left field.

I remember once my uncle Julie and his family were moving from Brooklyn. They lived two blocks from my house on East 93rd Street and Kings Highway and were moving to Flushing, Queens. I was in the house the day they were moving. The name of the moving company was the Bonnie Moving Company, owned and operated by Mr. Bonnie, who was telling my uncle and me about these baseball teams he had of all ages. I was about 10 years old then. Later, I joined a hardball team called the Bonnie Paws and I remembered Mr. Bonnie who owned the moving company that moved my uncle. Once, I refreshed his memory and he remembered the conversation we had and when I tried out for the team he welcomed me to the Bonnie Paws. I picked up my uniform and felt like a real professional.

I played for the Bonnie Paws for two years. They were good but never champions, not then anyway. As soon as I got older, I moved up to the Bonnie Bees. I played for the Bees for two years and I remember the last year I played for the Bees. We went undefeated and played for the New York City semi-finals in Babe Ruth Stadium in the Bronx. We won that game and went on to play for the city championship in the Polo Grounds. I believe that was in 1955. The Polo Grounds is where the New York Giants used to play before they moved to San Francisco. What a thrill that was for a young kid of fifteen playing for the championship on a professional baseball field. I remember being in the dressing room putting on my uniform and I looked out a small window and there was the field with its grass manicured so neat. I remember saying, "Look, fellows, look at this field" and everyone came over to the window for a look. It was beautiful. The dressing room was high up above the stands in left field. We got into our uniforms and were down on the field warming up. Thoughts kept going through my mind. "We have to win this game," I kept saying to myself. "We can't throw away a perfect season. Not now, we've come too far to lose now." Everything was riding on this one game. Our entire season, the undefeated season, we had to win this game. Our dugout was on the first base sideline.

We were in the dugout of the visiting teams that play at the Polo Grounds and I thought how many great players from all the teams had been in this dugout before me. I was walking in the footsteps of some of the greatest players in baseball. The entire Brooklyn Dodger team had been here so many times before. Duke Snyder, Peewee Reese, Roy "Campy" Campanella, Gil Hodges and so many others. There were about 600 fans in the stands, the largest crowd we ever played in front of. Our supporters were on the first base sideline, and theirs were on the third base side. Sitting along with the rest was my mother and my uncle Bernie.

The game started and I came to bat in the first inning with one run in, two on and two out. The pitcher just laid one in on me and I hit a line drive single over second base, which scored two runs. George, our pitcher, was flawless, as he had been all year. Their team was going down one after the other. In the fifth inning, some guy hits a long line drive to left field, my position. I took one step in and realized this ball is going over my head,

I had misjudged it badly. My friend Arnie ran over from center field yelling, "Third base, Al, third base." As it bounced off the wall in left field, I picked up the ball and threw it to third as hard as I could and I used every ounce of strength I had but the batter was safe on third. I felt terrible. The guy on third base was my responsibility and he scored on the next play. I was taken out of the game that inning. Not a good feeling, but it was the game of our lives and I could understand coach Ahern's decision. We won the game three to one and became city champions. That was a great day for me. Even though I didn't finish the game, it is still one day that I'll never forget. I don't think any one of us will. After the game, we all went for pizza on Mr. Bonnie. That was my last year of baseball.

I had got so involved with the gangs that not even baseball counted any more. At sixteen years old, I bought a car. In New York then, you had to be eighteen years old to get a license but by eighteen I already had owned five cars. The first car I bought was a 1949 Buick Road Master convertible. I had bought this car in the Bronx and had only driven a few miles my whole life and drove the car off the lot. My friend was with me to give me instructions that I never needed. I drove through the Bronx, got on the West Side Highway and was heading for the Brooklyn Battery Tunnel. I remember getting close to the toll booth at the tunnel and asking my friend if the car would fit through there. "Yeah," he said. I paid the toll and drove right through. In the tunnel, there were guys on the side speeding me up, telling me to drive faster by waving their arms and I remember thinking I must look eighteen years old. Having a car at that age was great. You had a car and you had the girls. I remember many times parking off the Belt Parkway to "Watch the submarine races," if you get my drift. We also would go to Coney Island almost every weekend. I loved Nathan's, the best hot dogs in town, with fries and a soda, 57 cents. I loved playing skeet-ball. Score enough points and you won your girl a teddy bear. Those were great days, I thought, having a car, running in gangs, staying out all night and not a responsibility in the world.

I remember once sitting in my house, with my brother and his friend talking in the living room. My brother's friend said, "In a few years you'll be ready for the draft." "Army," I said. "I ain't going to no Army." "Don't worry," my brother said. "We'll put needle marks in your arm and you'll tell them you're a drug addict." "Wait!" his friend said. "The day he goes, we'll give him a little so it will show in his urine." "No," my brother said, "we're not giving him no fix, just needle marks." I said, "The hell with the Army. I'd rather do six months in jail than go to the Army." I left the house soon after, leaving these two guys to figure out a way to keep me out of the Army.

From then on, I started to get more involved with gangs and started using drugs myself, although I knew I could never tell my brother. It was later on that my brother found out for sure that I was using. I would visit him in prison and he would confront me and he'd say, "Tony came in yesterday and said you're using. Is that true?" "No, man. Why would Tony say something like that?" I replied. Well, after a while, he knew I was lying because too many guys were coming in and telling him the same thing. One day I was in my house with one of my brother's friends getting high and my brother walks in. "What are you doing here?" I said. "You still have six weeks left to do." Well, my brother got out early. There had been a plane crash on Rikers Island in 1956 on a cold winter night. The plane took off from La Guardia Airport and crashed near the chicken farm of Rikers Island. My brother was one of the heroes that helped those poor people. The institution called on certain people. They used, I believe, the laundry crew because they had the biggest number of people and they needed the transportation crew because they needed the trucks and my brother was then clerk of transportation. For their bravery and hard work, everyone got six-month time cuts. My brother, only having six weeks left, was one of the first ones to leave and here he comes walking in my door with me having heroin on the table. "What are you doing?" he asked. "What do you think I'm doing? I'm getting high." "Relax," his friend Jackie said. "Come on get high with us." It didn't take him long to decide to get high again, all of thirty seconds. Then he said, "From now on, you hang out with me. Your friends are young and inexperienced and they don't know this game. You'll be safer with me," and then I got my wish. I was now partners with the guy I always looked up to, my brother.

We were now true partners, running together every day. We were committing small crimes, boosting mostly, suits out of department stores, cartons of cigarettes, which we sold to a store for two dollars a carton, but selling drugs was our favorite. Selling drugs was profitable and we didn't have to move. The money came to us. We made a great team. My brother had a knack for spotting the cops. "Don't look now, but the police are on the roof across the street," he said. As we turned the corner, I would look back and sure enough they were on the roof with binoculars. He was good at that. I had a knack for finding the drugs. When we went to buy some drugs and when the connection wasn't where he always was, I seemed to smell it, and I would get a sick feeling in my stomach. "He's around the corner," I would say. "How do you know that?" he says. "Come, I'll show you," and sure enough, the guy would be around the corner. This must have happened about five or six times and I never was wrong.

Once we were standing in front of this apartment building that we shared an apartment in, getting ready to walk to the bus stop and grab the bus to go buy our drugs. Two guys got out of a cab and walked inside the building. I saw them go into apartment number One as the front door was closing. "Come on, let's go," my brother said. "Stan, we don't have to go anywhere, these guys got something." "How do you know?" he asked. "Watch," I told him. I knocked on the door of apartment One and said, "Hey, fellas, I just moved into the building and I got a feeling you guys got something. You got enough to sell some?" "You use?" they asked. "Yeah, I use." I replied. "Roll up your sleeves and let me see your tracks (needle marks)," they said. I rolled up my sleeves and they said, "Come on in." My brother was amazed, but I was never wrong. We got high with these guys and when we walked upstairs, my brother said, "How the hell did you know they had something?" "I'm good," I said. Reality is that in situations like that I was always good at reading people. Remember me, the kid on the bus that would try to figure people out by the way they dressed, looked and walked.

There was something that was always troubling me. Although I was getting respect from my brother's friends, every time we walked up on the corner I would hear, "Here comes Rykoff and his kid brother," and I didn't like that. We were equals, I thought. I'm not the kid brother anymore. One day while high together, my brother asked me what I would do if we were stealing something and the cops rolled up, and I had a chance to get away but my brother didn't. Would I come back and try to help him or would I keep running? I said, "I'd probably come back for you." "Wrong answer," he said, "because there is no sense in us both going to jail. You should keep on running. I think we better split up," he says. "Split up?" I asked, "We're a team." "No," his answer was, "You do your thing and I'll do mine and we'll meet every day around the same time and pool the money." "O.K. if that's the way you want it, we will do it your way," I said to my brother.

Each day we would split up and do our own thing and it became a competition with me. I wasn't going to be called "Rykoff's kid brother" anymore so if he came up with fifty dollars, I came up with seventy-five. We had a phone booth that we used to call each other at around 2:00 P.M. "How'd you do?" I would ask. "Got twenty-five dollars." "I'll meet you in an hour," I would say because I had to beat those twenty-five dollars and, in most cases, I did. My trick had worked. My brother who was so proud of me was telling his friends what a good thief I was and soon we became the Rykoff brothers instead of Rykoff and his kid brother. Soon I was running with his friends as much as he was; they wanted me around, I was good at what I did. Nothing big, all small time crimes, but I was good at it. Now I was hanging out with the big guys in the neighborhood, guys I knew since I was a child but I was always looked at like the kid. I wasn't the kid anymore, I was into it as much as they were and, like my brother, I was on top of things.

I started using by smoking pot at age 14 or 15, did that for a short time, then went on to pills and most times it was pills and pot. Then I started using heroin. When I started using drugs, me and three friends would chip in a dollar and a quarter each, four of us, and we would buy a 5-dollar bag of heroin and snort it (Using a small straw to get it up your nose) and we would get high and walk for hours. Just walking and walking, sometimes throwing up on the way, but that didn't bother us at all. Soon I was using almost every day, but life changed for me then. Here, rather then feeling stupid, I was sharp, I was fast and I became a leader rather than a follower. I was the man in charge. I was the guy who came up with the schemes. I was the guy who had all the connections and I was the guy getting all the respect and I liked it. Yes, I was my brother with the guys my age. He had taught me well and I learned my lessons. Here I knew the game; here I knew how to get the respect. Jail wasn't a problem. Once you're over the initial shock of where you are and realize the reality, then you're O.K. If you're a stand-up guy, you have no problems. I was in and out of Rikers Island so many times I thought they were going to put my statue in centerfield or name a cell block after me.

I was there in 1956 for driving without a license. In 1958, I was in for scofflaw (not paying your traffic tickets). That was a strange arrest. The police came to my house because there was a warrant for my arrest for not paying a speeding ticket. I was down at the police station and it was around 4:00 P.M. and the shifts were changing. Police were coming in and out of the room I was in. One cop said, "What do you have this guy for?" "Not paying a ticket," the other cop said. The first cop answered, "What ticket, the one I gave him?" "Did you give him a speeding ticket?" "No, I think it was a red light." Another cop walked in and the conversation was just about the same. Finally, about six or eight cops had the same conversation and the arresting officer said, "O.K. how many tickets do you have?" I said, "Look, you got a warrant for one speeding ticket. Let's just worry about that one ticket." He laughed at me and said, "Once we get to court, all the tickets will show up so how many do you have?" "Thirteen," I answered. I seem to get one every Friday night. I wound up getting thirty days for not paying my tickets and my license was suspended for one year.

My record was as follows:
1953, bringing the gun to school (three weeks)
1958, scofflaw (30 days)
1960, possession of a hypodermic needle (30 days)
1961, possession of a hypodermic needle (six months)
1962, drug possession (six months)
1962, possession of a hypodermic needle (six months)
1963, possession of a hypodermic needle (six months)
1964, possession of a hypodermic needle (six months)
1965 through 66, Grand Larceny (three years)
Each sentence spent on Rikers Island

You have to ask yourself, how many times does he have to get arrested for the same charge before he learns? Well, five of those arrests were because my mother would call the police on me. She would find my needles and call the police. She thought I would be safer in jail then outside using drugs and she was probably right. It must have been very hard for her but I was the baby of the family and she didn't want to lose me.

I remember the first time I did a six month's sentence on Rikers Island, my brother came to visit me and he was smiling. "What's up?" I asked, "Fill me in so I can laugh also." "Remember once in the living room you said you'd rather do six months than go to the army for two years?" "Yeah, I remember that." "Well, your draft notice came and I sent them a letter telling them you're here doing six months for drugs and they sent you a 4-f card. Watch what you ask for," he said. "It may come to pass." "May come to pass?" I said. "It did come to pass" and we laughed together.

Rikers Island is a very large island located in the East River in New York City. At one point, it's about 500 feet from LaGuardia Airport. Access to the island was by ferry from 134th St. in the Bronx. Now, I understand, access is over a bridge from Astoria, Queens. It's a city in itself. At one time, and maybe still today, it also was used to grow all the trees that you see along the highways and in city parks. Why not? They had the room and the prisoners would do the work. Usually they put the guys that got into trouble a lot on these labor gangs. Once I remember asking Capt. Adler, the assignment officer, to be put on Labor Two. He asked, "Why would you want to go to Labor Two?" and I told him that most of the guys from my neighborhood were on Labor Two. So he did and I was transferred from the receiving block to the cellblock that houses Labor Two. Capt. Adler was a good officer and always tried to make things easier for inmates.

Labor Two wasn't that bad a job. During the summer months we would go out into the fields, wet ourselves down with water and just lay in the sun. I never had such a great tan in my life. We would watch the planes land and take off always wondering where they were going and where they came from. Girls passing the island on boats would always wave hello. They really weren't close enough for us to see them but we could tell they were women and they were waving and that would always put a smile on my face.

Soon we referred to getting arrested as "being rescued." We knew that the longer you stayed out there, the sooner you were going to die. Even knowing that didn't stop us; Rikers Island was a revolving door. Once you've been there and come back, it's always the same faces. Nobody left and stayed out unless they died. Not my crowd anyway. My brother and I were always going in and out of prison. Once I remember being out two weeks. Got out on Tuesday, October 9th and was back in on Tuesday, Oct 23rd. I believe that was in 1962. Came out again, and two weeks to the day my friend Tony and I found ourselves in the Canarsie police station. We had broken into a car that was filled with suits and other clothing. The car was parked in back of the Beth-El Hospital (since renamed) on East 98th St. We broke the window and cops from three precincts surrounded us. We were right on the borderline of these three precincts. One cop told me that the reason they were there was because they saw Tony and wanted him. Somehow they located the guy who owned the car. He had been in the hospital visiting someone before he left town. He refused to press charges, stating that he was leaving town and not coming back. We were released.

Later that night, Tony and I were walking on Saratoga Ave, near Riverdale Ave, and here comes the police again. These guys were from the Brownsville police station but had been on the scene when Tony and I broke into the car and they thought we had escaped. They searched us, handcuffed us, and called to find out how we got away. Once they found out we hadn't escaped and since neither of us had anything illegal on us, they had to release us. I said, "Tony, I did six months, was out two weeks, got busted and back for another six months. Today I'm home two weeks again. I'll see you tomorrow because I'm going home and make sure I can last more then two weeks this time." Tony laughed and we went in separate directions. It's not easy leaving jail and going right back in again. The hardest part are your friends. "Hey, where were you, in the hospital, or were you in the bing (solitary confinement)?" or you get the wise-ass who says, "Did you at least have one good meal?" Reality is, it's all in fun but you know you left yourself open for it.

Getting arrested isn't fun. When you're questioned in the police station and they want information that they know you have, some cops will beat you till they get tired and some know not to waste their time. In New York, at least when I was running the streets, when you got arrested you spent the night in a cell in the police station sleeping on a wooden bench, if you can sleep, and in the morning a paddy wagon takes you to court and from there you go to jail. I remember once getting arrested in the Canarsie area but they had no cells in that police station so they took me over to spend the night on Empire Blvd. at the police station there. In the morning I was out of the cell putting on my shoelaces, which they take away from you along with your belt, and I was kneeling down. All of a sudden, I get a hard slap on the head. I looked up and it was Officer Schultz, a police officer that I had known since I was a kid. "I see you graduated," he said, meaning that now I was using drugs. Before, it was fighting and stealing a little. "What can I say?" I answered. He once arrested my brother when my brother was very young and had to go explain to my mother. She became hysterical and I think he said, "Never again." He used to catch me fighting, kick me in the butt and send me home but he never arrested me for anything. As I was walking out of the station-house, he asked the arresting officer, "Did my friend help you with any information?" The cop laughed and said, "Your friend, huh?" Mr. Schultz answered back in a stern voice, "That's right! This kid is a personal friend of mine." The arresting officer said, "He told me he would die before giving me any information." As I walked out the door, I turned back to my friend who nodded in agreement and winked at me. He knew I would be O.K. in jail.

I went to court and found myself in Raymond Street Jail that night and I got a cell by myself. I was facing about three years and, after a few days, they gave me a cell partner. He walks in as I'm laying in my bunk relaxing. He throws his sheets and blankets on the bed and starts to pace back and forth, back and forth, back and forth. With the bars on one side and the toilet and sink on the other, you only had about three or four feet to pace but he wouldn't stop. He was driving me crazy pacing for about a half hour. He never said a word, just paced and paced. "What are you here for?" I asked. "Child support," he replied. I jumped up off my bunk and said, "Child support, you f--king bum. You come in here with a bullshit charge and you're going to drive me crazy by pacing and pacing. I'm facing forty years dummy, so get in your bunk and shut the hell up." He got in his bunk and didn't say a word. About twenty minutes later, someone must have paid the fine for him and he got out. I'm sure he had some stories to talk about when he got home being in with this criminal who was facing forty years. Reality is that I was only facing three years but this guy was driving me crazy and I knew I had to scare him off to stop him from pacing. After he left, I broke the other bed and every time they brought me a cell partner I told the guard the bunk was broken. I stayed alone for my entire stay there. Sure I could be considered a jerk for doing what I did to that guy but this guy was getting me crazy and I had problems of my own to think about. Fact is, if you can't do time, don't put yourself in a position to get arrested. There used to be a sign on the wall of a pool room I used to hang out in and it read, "If you can't pay, don't play."

I was also a very lucky guy. I remember once my friend and I beat this other guy up and the next thing I heard was that his father was looking for us and had a gun. He caught my friend one night and had my friend on his knees praying for mercy; then he pistol-whipped him. Every time I would walk on Legion St. and Riverdale Ave. where we hung out, I would hear, "Wow, you're lucky. That guy's father was just here looking for you." Or I would hear, "Five minutes after you left, his father showed up." This went on for weeks. Finally, this guy's father called me on the phone and said, "You hear what I did to your friend?" "Yeah, I heard. So what?" "I'm going to do the same to you. I'm going to put a gun to your head and have you beg for mercy." "You are?" I said. "Let me tell you something. You pull a gun any place near me and I'm going to take it away from you, stick it up your ass and pull the trigger. Who do you think you're talking to with your threats, some bum on the streets?" "You got nerve," he said. "Did you ever think of becoming a boxer?" This idiot who five minutes ago was looking to put a gun to my head and make me beg for mercy now likes me and wants to train me to become a fighter. Was I so tough? No. He was on the other end of the phone. I could have said anything I wanted to. Had I seen him with the gun, I may have run faster than a racehorse but being on the phone afforded me the opportunity to act and sound as tough as I wanted to. I never heard from or saw the father again.

Another lucky time I had was in 1963. I had this pharmacist who had a drugstore four blocks away from my house. He used to sell me needles and the barbiturates "two in all." One day I got him to sell me Dilaudid. Dilaudid taken intravenously is stronger than heroin. It's a pure drug. I walked into the store to get some pills and he said to me, "You look sick." I wasn't sick but since he said that I played along, wanting him to think I was. "Yeah, Lou, sick like a dog. Why don't you sell me some Dilaudid?" I told the pharmacist. "How many you need?" he asked. "Ten would do the trick," I replied. He walked into the back and returned in a few minutes. "Here's the pills (two in all)" he said and I said, "Here's your two dollars." Then he handed me the ten Dilaudid. "How much do I owe you for this, Lou?" "Ten dollars," Lou said. "O.K. I owe it to you," I said and I walked out.

I didn't have any money on me but before he found that out, I wanted the Dilaudid in my hands. My friend Tony was waiting for me around the corner. "Let's go to my house," I said. "You won't believe what I got." Well, this was the number one drug that people who use heroin want from a drugstore so it wasn't hard for Tony to guess. We went to my house, got high, and I said that we have to come up with money right now. Tony and I walked to Flatbush Ave., four blocks away from where I now was living on Martense St. and Nostrand Ave. We walked to a store that sold T.V.'s. Tony kept the clerk busy while I grabbed a T.V. and ran out the door. We knew a guy that lived a few blocks away that would take stolen stuff. We sold the T.V. for forty dollars and I walked right back into the drug store. I told Lou, "Here's your ten dollars and give me thirty more." He did. I now was in business.

Every day I would meet Lou when he opened the store and I would buy 160 Dilaudid from him. They were costing me a dollar apiece and I was selling them for two dollars each or three for five dollars. What a bargain. I would sell around eighty and shoot about eighty and I had a habit that I had hoped I never would have to kick. This went on for about four months. One day I went to visit my brother who was awaiting trial in Raymond Street Jail. "You got problems," he told me when I saw him. "What are you talking about?" I asked. Mursh came in yesterday and told me the Rackets Bureau questioned him about you. "The Rackets Bureau, what the hell do they want with me?" I asked. "They know you're dealing Dilaudid. You got to stop," he said. "Stop, but I can't stop. Do you know what it would cost me if I went back to heroin? Stan, I'm shooting eighty pills a day. It would cost me around two hundred dollars just to keep from being sick every day, let alone getting high." My brother said, "Al, if the Rackets Bureau gets their hands on you, you won't see daylight for thirty years. They're like the FBI. You can't beat them." Well, I didn't stop, I kept going, and day after day I would meet Lou when he opened the store. Day after day I was selling eighty and shooting eighty. I felt safe. I was selling mostly to my brother's friends who now became my friends and these were old-timers in the business of using drugs. Guys I knew to be stand-up guys who were in and out of prison and never ratted on anyone.

One day Mel, a guy that was my brother's friend and I had known since I was a young kid, called me on the phone. Mel was a steady customer. Every day he would buy from me. "You got anything?" he asked. "No, but I will have it soon." As I walked out of my building to go to the drugstore, Mel was walking in. "Come on, Mel, take a walk with me," I said. Mel was nervous, very nervous, and I confronted him and asked, "What's happening that you're so nervous?" "I'm not nervous, I'm sick, need a fix," he said. "No problem," I said. "Give me a few minutes and I'll have you fixed in no time." We got a block from the drug store. "Wait here, Mel. I'll be right back." Mel was married with a family and designed submarines for the government. He had a very good-paying job and a very responsible job. I got back in about ten minutes. "Give me the stuff and let me go," he said. "No, Mel, come to my house and get high with me." "No, no," he said. "I got to go, got to get back to work." "Mel, I'm not letting you walk away sick, come up to my house or go someplace else for your drugs," and I refused to give him anything. He came to my house and I cooked it up for him and we both got high. The following day, he came back and still was very nervous, saying he was sick again and again I would not let him walk away sick and again I cooked up his fix. A few days later, I decided to go into Kings County Hospital to kick my habit. It had gotten out of hand and my brother was on my back about the Rackets Bureau.

When I got out of the hospital, I went back to the drugstore and saw the druggist. "You ratted me out," he said. The druggist had gotten arrested. "Are you crazy?" I answered. "I never ratted on anyone," I told him, in no uncertain terms. "Lou, I should wreck your store for you even thinking that way about me but when you go to court you will find out who ratted you out. When do you go to court?" He told me. "Fine, I'll be in the next day." Two months later, a day after his court date, I showed up at the store. "Do you know a guy named Mel?" he said. It seems the two days that Mel was overly nervous and said he was sick was because he brought the cops with him and they followed me to the store. I used to check to see if I was followed but these guys were smarter than me. I never knew they were there. I would have gotten arrested also, but for me to get arrested Mel would have had to produce the drug. He probably had marked money and may have even worn a wire. He gives the cops the drugs and they pick me up with the marked money and then I don't have a leg to stand on. Because I was a nice guy and wouldn't let him walk away sick saved me a whole lot of trouble. Selling drugs at that time was punishable by 15 years in state prison and who knows if they would have added racketeering charges because I was getting it from a druggist. It really pays to be nice.

In 1964 I was arrested for grand larceny, burglar tools and unlawful entry, and was facing about 13 years in prison, but remember, I was a schemer and I would find a way to get out of this. My brother was doing a small sentence on Harts Island and I was transferred from Raymond Street Jail to a jail in Queens because Raymond St. was too crowded. I got a letter from my brother three days after my arrest. You can't believe the power of the grapevine in prison. Once you walk in the door, the word goes out to every prison in New York. It's amazing. I remember being in the receiving room at Rikers Island taking my shower and getting dressed into my prison clothes. This was my first day in the penitentiary. I walked into Two Block, the receiving block, and as I walked in I was greeted by my brother's friends, who knew I was coming in that day. I remember holding my blankets, sheets and pillowcase, and looking around. This was it, big time prison, I had moved to the top of the chain. Looking up at the tiers, three tiers high, 26 cells on a tier, and four sections in a cellblock. It was a scary sight. What goes on here? How do I act? Where do I start?

With two men in a cell, that brings the population to more than 600 in each cellblock. The walls were three stories high with windows that open out but only a few inches so that no one can escape. "Just like the movies," I thought. Soon I was assigned a cell and I was locked in. "Rather small," I thought. Pale green in color. Two bunk beds attached to the wall by screws, a small sink with cold water only. Next to the sink was the toilet. No toilet seat and in the cold winter months using that toilet, well, I hope you'll never have to experience it. Out from the wall was a little table and seat. There was a small cabinet attached to the wall and that was it. My new house, a small dingy lit cell. "Damn, this is where I spend my time," I thought. This is now my home.

Soon the tier man showed up at my cell and asked me, "You Rykoff's brother?" "Yeah," I said. The tier man said, "This is for you," about 50 dollars worth of commissaries. "This is from Joe in Eight Block a friend of your brother's. This is from Phil in Six Block" and so on and so forth. Guys I didn't know, names I never heard but they were friends of my brother and this was the respect my brother had owned. Also what came to me were pressed pants and shirts, starched to the hilt. I had to pull the pants' legs apart to get into them. My starched shirt had three creases down the back. I remember walking out of my cell for the first time and dressed in my pressed cloths and I remember my friend Louie the Pimp asking me who my tailor was. This was what came out of being a stand-up guy. This is what all the schemes were about, all the fights and all the manipulations. People knew who you were. Now, being Stan's brother was good once again. It was like that every time I got there, only now it was on my own reputation, not my brother's. I had proved myself on the streets and in prison.

In return for the commissary sent to me, I would also send packages to people I knew that just came in. Prison is hard enough so friends always look out for one another. Not only is it the right thing to do, but once again, our way of saying, "You can't hurt us, we pull together." You have to know how to do your time. Doing time isn't easy; there is tension all around you day after day and there are two ways to do time. One way, the way my brother did his time, was knowing everyone, being friendly with everyone, but having only a handful of close friends. Then there was the way I did time, which also involves knowing everyone, being friendly with everyone but at the same time I ran with gangs, in packs, like animals. My brother's way was smarter and safer. My way brought more tension, fights and problems. Later on I learned my brother's way. I had my reputation, everyone knew me and now I could relax and get some good friends, play bridge and get this over with.

Rikers Island, the main unit beyond the control center has this very long hallway with a yellow line down the center. Everyone walks in two's with guards in the middle. You're counted almost every time your walk through a door. You're counted again with every shift change, at 8:00 A.M., 4:00 P.M. and 12 midnight. The long corridor houses cell blocks on both sides. Cellblocks 1-2-4-6 and 8 are on one side and blocks 3-5 and 7 on the other side. Two large mess halls are on the odd side of the hall and across from the mess hall you have your churches and synagogue. Rikers Island was built to house 2,800 men. When I was there, we were housing 6,000, so you could imagine the crowded condition, which creates lots of tension. In those days, we had the reformatory, the reception center and the penitentiary but today I understand they built more buildings and even have a women's prison there. I had a 6-month sentence for my second drug arrest: possession of a hypodermic needle. I was about 21 years old. I had been on Rikers Island twice before but because of my age I was on the reformatory side, in a dormitory setting. I had done 30 days for scofflaw (not paying my traffic tickets) and my first drug arrest got me another 30 days, both spent in the reformatory on Rikers Island.

I had remembered once a friend of my brother's walking into the pool room we hung out in on Dumont and Saratoga Ave's. He asked me if I ever got arrested for drugs and at that time I still hadn't. I remember like it was yesterday. He said, "Well, once that first one comes they all start coming after that." He was so right and jail can be very cruel. I remember going to the mess hall to eat. The tray I picked was dirty so I put it on top of the tray rack and took another tray and the guard says to me, "What's wrong with the other tray?" "It's dirty sir." "It's dirty?" he replied. "In the street you ate off newspaper. Put that tray back and use the other one." I put the tray back, looked at him and said, "I'd rather not eat." I walked into the mess hall and skipped that meal. That happened to me twice.

I remember the first time I was in Raymond Street Jail, my brother sent me a message to meet him in Jewish services on Friday. After services were over, we all were looking out the window and someone whistled at this woman that was walking by. The guard, known to us as a hack, came running up to me screaming about me whistling out the window. It wasn't me who whistled. The truth is, I never learned how to whistle, but I couldn't tell him who it was, and the punk didn't have enough heart to own up to it so I took the abuse like a man. In this prison you were locked in 22 hours a day. You came out for 20 minutes for each meal. The meals were so fast that you had to make sandwiches and take them back to your cell. Ever eat a bean sandwich? You got out of your cell again once a day for a walk. They would walk you in a circle in the yard with guards always looking down from the towers.

This was a prison in Brooklyn used for inmates still going to court. My brother was "locking" on the tier opposite me but down the other end of his tier. My brother and his friends would line up for chow at the end of their line and me and my friends would line up at the beginning of our line so my tier followed my brother's line into the mess hall and it gave my brother and me a chance to eat together. I remember walking to the mess hall and seeing a friend of mine in his cell. He had just got there. "What do you have?" I asked. "Burglary," he said. "They got you right?" I asked. "Yeah," he said. "They caught me inside the place." "Then it's not burglary," I said. "It's unlawful entry," and I threw him a pack of cigarettes that I had in my pocket. As I got closer to the mess hall, some hack pulled me out of line. "Face the wall," he said. "What's happening?" I asked. "Face the f--king wall; you stepped out of line," he said. So I faced the wall till everyone finished eating then I was told to walk to the end of the tier. This was my first time in this jail and I was only a kid at 21 years old. At the end of the tier were six hacks just waiting for me. "He's the guy that whistled out the window," one said. They grabbed me and started beating me, knocking me to the floor and proceeded to kick me while I was down. There is nothing I could do. Fight back and they have the right to kill you in their defense so you take it like a man and don't utter a word. Your way of saying, "The hell with you." I was walked back to my cell and I was so mad. Think about that. I took one step out of line and six guards were beating me and I thought to myself, "They call me the criminal." The old Raymond St. Jail has since been torn down and the space added to the hospital down the block. From what I understand, it was built during the Civil War.

Jail became a routine part of being an addict. You do your time, get out and some months later, (if you manage to stay out that long) you're back in jail again. But getting back to this arrest. I was now facing about 13 years for the grand larceny, burglar tools and unlawful entry. My brother wrote me telling me to apply for an Article Nine. An Article Nine is that you plead guilty to a misdemeanor, serve three months in a mental hospital and then you're placed on probation. We knew that addicts can't make a probation, not with needle marks on their arms and drugs in their urine but having a misdemeanor was punishable by only three years in prison, not the 13 years I was facing. I applied for the Article Nine and was turned down.

A month or two later, Judge Julius Helfand summoned me to Brooklyn Supreme Court. I found out later that my mother did a lot of talking to people, talking and begging because her baby was facing thirteen years. They called my case and the judge asked me if I had ever heard of a program by the name of Daytop Lodge. When I told him no, he remanded me for counsel. An attorney came to the cell behind the court to tell me about this program called Daytop. He told me they had wall-to-wall carpeting and color T.V. I found out since that what this guy was telling me was the worst type of data that could have been told to anyone but

I guess he just wanted to entice me with these goodies. He should have been telling me the truth. "It's not going to be easy, but you'll have the chance to change you're entire life around and become a more productive person." He also told me that the judge would have to lower the charge to a misdemeanor, because Daytop didn't accept felony cases.

Those were the magic words. I now knew I turned thirteen years into three years. The attorney and I talked for about 20 minutes and later I was summoned back to court. The judge asked if I would be interested in going to a program like Daytop. "Yes, your honor. It's time I got some help" was my reply. I pleaded guilty to a misdemeanor to cover the burglar tools and the grand larceny and the judge said I should go to the probation department and they will give me carfare and directions to Staten Island where Daytop was located. "I can't leave, your honor," I said. "I have an unlawful entry case stemming from the same indictment in the lower courts." The judge got furious and asked the court clerk to check. "Yes, your honor, he's right. There is another case in the lower court." Judge Helfand remanded me back to jail for one week while he cleared this up. I was so happy because now the thirteen years was gone; Daytop, as far as I knew, was an eighteen-month program. This was great, I got out from under that thirteen years and that was my main concern. I wasn't looking for help, I didn't want help, and I liked being a drug addict. It was easy for me and I was comfortable in that role.

I saw a very large picture of the Verrazano Bridge, which had just opened, in a magazine. It was the centerfold and the photo was on both sides making one large photo. I took it out of the magazine and hung it on my wall in the cell. I knew I had to cross this bridge to get to Daytop.I returned to court the following week and was told by Judge Helfand that the unlawful entry was thrown out. "You're cleared to go to Daytop," he said. Being the schemer that I was, the first thing I thought about was that if the unlawful entry was thrown out, how can they prove I was in the building to commit the crime but I didn't have enough time to think this through and I was also smart enough to know you can't beat these people. If they want you, they get you. "Yes, your honor, thank you very much," I said. I was placed on probation and given directions and I was on my way to Daytop. As I said, I wasn't looking for help with my problems. I liked being a drug addict, change scared me and it was something I thought might be later down the road but certainly not now. The only thing I wanted from Daytop was to get out from under a thirteen-year sentence.

Daytop at the time was located at 450 Bayview Ave, Staten Island. I crossed the newly opened Verrazano Bridge. To me, it was a beautiful bridge. To me, everything was beautiful. I was just out of jail and it was a nice sunny day. I remember walking down Bayview Ave. from where the bus left me. It was a long dirt road. It seemed like I was walking forever. Then, at the end of the block was this very large beautiful house on top of a hill.

I walked in and was given a chair to sit in and I sat for about two hours. The reason for that is twofold. First, to make you understand that they don't need you, you need them, and also to get an idea of how the house works. Some guys were cleaning, others walking around with papers. I could see people walking in and out of the kitchen and, in short, there was a lot of activity. After about two hours, I was called in for an interview. There were about six people in my interview sitting in a semi-circle on couches and living room chairs and I in the middle on a wooden chair. They first asked what I was doing there. I told them that the court sent me. "For what purpose?" they asked. "To get some help." "Help with what?" was the reply. "Help with this drug problem I have." I said. "Drug problem?" they asked. "Drugs are not a problem." "It is for me," I said. "Is the drug the problem or are you the problem?" they asked. "If there were drugs on the table would it be a problem? No. The person that picks it up has the problem and right now you would pick it up. Isn't that right, Al?" Damn, I was never up against anything like this before and I was getting confused. Questions were coming from all sides. "Think you're a man, Al?" they asked. "Yeah, I'm a man," I replied. "When you got arrested, who was the first person you called?" they asked. "I called my mother," I replied. "You call your mommy, very much like a baby would do, mommy, mommy help me," they said in a sarcastic voice. "It's not like that," I said. "Sure it is, you just can't see that. You think you're a man because you have hair on your chest but you're no man," they remarked. This interview was getting harder and harder for me and it went on for about an hour like this. I wanted to get out of there, but it was back to jail I would be going, so I stuck it out a little longer. They were insistent that I admit I'm not a man and I had refused to do that so they sat me back on the chair to think.

The chair was located by a desk at one end of the living room. Now sitting at the desk was my friend Buddy who I had gotten high with a few times. Buddy said in a whisper, "We're not supposed to be talking." I said, "Buddy, these guys are crazy, want me to say I'm not a man." "That's the only way you're going to get in here and if you leave you'll do every day of the three years," he answered. "Damn!" I said. "They got me uptight." He said, "Just be cool and in a while I'll tell them you're ready." Buddy wasn't supposed to be telling me that, but Buddy wasn't one to follow the rules. Needless to say, Buddy left a few days later, but Buddy did tell them about a half hour later that I was ready and I walked into the office and still it took me about 30 minutes to tell them I wasn't a man. They asked what I had to say and I said, "You're right." "Right about what?" they asked. "Right about what you said," was my reply. "What did we say?" they asked. "You know what you said," I replied. "No, refresh our memories," they answered. "You said I wasn't a man," I told them. "What do you think, Al?" they asked. "I think you're right." "About what, Al?" "About what you said." This went on and on for about ten minutes and finally they were laughing and soon I started laughing as well. I knew what they wanted and I knew I had to give it to them. It was time to give up my image, to say the one thing I thought I would never have to say. "O.K. I'm not a man," I said. "Welcome to Daytop" they told me.

The director, I found out later, wanted me in Daytop. There was another guy that I knew in the interview whose name is Freddy. Freddy had told the director he knew me from the streets, and the director asked him about me before the interview. Freddy told him I'd be a tough cookie and if he changes me he's really doing his job. So according to Freddy, who told me this years later, I became a challenge to the director.

After I was accepted, I was taken around to meet everyone and was told that if I knew anyone, I had to tell them and then I wouldn't be able to talk to that person. We would be put on a ban. That's done because what would we be talking about, the old days, getting high, sharing stories about guys we knew, nothing but negative things. As I was walking around the house with this guy who was introducing me to everyone, I saw my friend Johnny. "Johnny wouldn't say anything," I thought. "He's good people." As we were introduced, I said, "Glad to meet you, Johnny." Johnny turned to the other guy and said, "I know Al from jail." "What the hell is going on here?" I thought. "What type of place is this?" I had an interview none like I've ever seen before. My friend Freddy confronting me in the interview and was asking me if I thought I was a man. Buddy telling me that we were not supposed to be talking and now Johnny turning on me the way he did. I just couldn't figure things out. Buddy and I got high together. Freddy and I also got high together and were from the same neighborhood. Johnny and I were in jail twice together. What the hell is going on here?

The following day I was put on the service crew. The service crew was responsible for the cleaning of the house, all but the individual bedrooms that were cleaned by the people that lived in those rooms. So here I was cleaning windows. The facility had so many doors with French windows in them. They were 6" X 6" squares and I was cleaning all of them. I was dusting tables, lamps, high ledges, low ledges, everything. I never lifted a finger at home to clean anything and here I was washing windows and dusting and still unable to figure out what was going on in this program. I continued on trying to figure this place out. I still couldn't talk to Freddy or Johnny and Buddy had left the program. There were so many times that I wanted to leave but I was thinking of time. Eighteen months here opposed to three years in jail. Everyone seemed to be into the program except me. What were they seeing that I wasn't? Was I missing the boat or were all these guys crazy?

We were going to group encounter sessions three times a week, Monday, Wednesday and Friday evenings. Those sessions are geared for you to learn about you, to talk about yourself, your feelings, your thoughts, your needs and your wants. They're also used to confront a person who may have hurt your feelings or done something you didn't like. The purpose of that is for you to control your feelings till the proper time to let it out and that was in the group encounter sessions. Addicts aren't very good at controlling their feelings. I didn't like these group encounter sessions. There you became vulnerable, open for all to see, and that was something I had trouble dealing with. I was learning so much about myself, about my inadequacies, my fears, my hang-ups, my way of thinking, my values or lack of values, morals and convictions, that I really got scared. For the first time, I was seeing myself as another person and four months later I left Daytop.

This was a violation of my probation and now I was on the run. I took a small hotel room in midtown Manhattan and, of course, went right back to using drugs. One day this police officer grabbed me in midtown, took me into a hall and searched me. I had nothing on me and he let me go but not before telling me, "If I ever see you around here again, I'm locking you up." One day, a few weeks later, I was walking with my brother on 48th St. and Broadway in midtown and here comes this same cop who pulls my brother and me into another hallway. He searches my brother and finds nothing. He then searched me and found drugs, so it was off to the police station we went. In the station house, I kept insisting that this guy I was with didn't know I had any drugs on me. My brother had given them a phony name. In those days there were only fingerprints but no computers and it took a few days for your prints to come back. Well, I always wanted to be like my brother and here we were handcuffed together and then put in the same cell. It now wasn't such a good feeling to be like my brother but I was an addict and this is the life addicts live. I also knew that, aside from the possession-of-heroin charge, I would also have the violation-of-probation charge. I was now looking at about four years in prison. Thirty-two days I was out of Daytop and now back in jail once again and with a possession charge and a probation violation warrant.

The next day my brother and I went to court and I told the judge that this guy had no idea I was holding any drugs on me. My brother was released and I went to city prison Manhattan (the Tombs). A week later, I was taken to Brooklyn Supreme Court to face Judge Helfand again and to be sentenced for my probation violation. I was given an indefinite term of up to three years. I was brought back to Manhattan to await sentencing on the possession charge.

The day I went to court on my possession charge my brother was there sitting with the spectators. The Judge sentenced me to one year in the New York City Penitentiary. (Rikers Island) My brother yelled to me, "That's illegal." Then it dawned on me. I turned to the judge and said, "Your honor, last week I was sentenced by Justice Julius Helfand in Brooklyn Supreme Court to an indefinite term of up to three years. That's a rehabilitation sentence. You cannot punish me after I am rehabilitated." He asked the court clerk to check the records and they found that I was right. He had to have given me that sentence before I got the three years, then I would have had to do the one year sentence and "turn around" as we call it and do the three-year sentence, but once I was considered rehabilitated he can't punish me. My one-year sentence was suspended. I turned to my brother and nodded, "Thanks" as they were taking me out of the courtroom.

The officer in charge of the prisoners said, "He cut you loose, huh?" and I said, "Yeah." Obviously the guard wasn't paying attention. "Well, I have to take you upstairs to check for warrants." he said. As we were walking upstairs I said, "I have no warrants, I was only out thirty-two days" and he was just ready to let me go when the officer in the back said, "Who you got there, Rykoff? Bring him up here. He's got three years hanging over his head." The cop put me in a separate cell and once again I knew what was coming. See, if you escape on a police officer he loses 30 days pay and this guy was quite mad. About 10 minutes later the officer opened the cell and walked in. "I should kick your ass," he said. I told him that he could do whatever he wanted, but "Don't turn your back on me because I'm gone." "You're a crazy bastard," he said as he walked out of the cell.

The next day I was back on Rikers Island, # 265-3040, the two for the type of sentence I had, an indefinite term, 65 for the year and 3040 was my number. Well, here I was again back in the New York City penitentiary. "Would this ever end?" I asked myself. I was getting tired of prison life and here I was with a brand new three-year sentence. In about the last six or seven years, I had spent five and a half in prison. In and out, in and out. It was getting crazy already. I remember laying on my bed in my cell and thinking, "How nice it would be if I could take my brain out of my head, put it on the table and tighten some screws, add some oil, put the brain back in my head and never have to worry about drugs or jail again," but it's just not that simple. I knew I had the chance in Daytop but that was the hard way to change. I was looking for an easier way and there was none.

A few months later, I was working in Two Block as a tier man. The tier man gives out the toilet paper to the cells in his area, passes out the toilet brush and the mop in the morning and mops his tier. The guard in charge of the cellblock must search 10 cells a day at random. The guard we had was driving me crazy. Every day he would search my cell and what a mess he made. He ripped everything apart. You get back to your cell and everything was on the floor. Your sheets, pillowcase, toothbrush and paste. Your soap, writing paper, stamps cookies, your cup, everything you have in your cabinet, everything. The cell was upside down. He was getting me crazy. Every day, day after day, I was being harassed by this hack till one day he overstepped his bounds.

I had three writs in my cell. One I was trying to get back to court for re-sentencing in the hopes of getting a shorter sentence. I had another writ because they never gave me credit for the four months I served in Queens before going to Daytop and another, which I can't remember. Each writ is about 140 to 160 pages and one day I found them all over my cell and I just went crazy. I was in the cell, the door still open and the hack walks by. "You stupid son of a bitch!" I yelled. "You have been harassing me for months. What right do you have to touch my legal papers? You're an asshole, don't you know the law? This is my freedom you're f--king with." He was yelling back and cursing me as well. "Come out of the cell!" he yelled. "No, you f--king asshole, you come in," I said. The reason for that is the door is so narrow that if I walk through the door he gets the first punch and he was holding this big ring of keys with his arm back ready to swing. "Get your ass in here," I yelled. "I'm going to f--k you up." By now half the cellblock is standing around and I can see my friends trying to tell me to cool it. No, there was no cooling it. This man overstepped his bounds and by law he's not allowed to touch my legal papers and by now I had gone past the point of no return so there was no stopping me. This argument went on for about five minutes. I wouldn't come out and he wouldn't come in. He walked away.

It was time to lock in and my friends came over and I gave them all my stuff to hold for me. I knew I was going to solitary confinement. I started handing my stuff to my friends, cigarettes, candy, cookies, toothpaste and brush, writing paper, stamps and envelopes, razor and mirror and whatever else I had, and I waited. The four o'clock shift came on and still nothing. They opened the cells for chow and my friends were surprised I was still there. They were surprised that I was still alive. For an offence like this, you're usually in big trouble and while in solitary you're subject to get beaten often. The next day I saw the same guard. He looked at me and I looked at him but nothing was said. In my head, I had won. He had harassed me for a long time and I made a fool of him in front of half the cellblock and there are six hundred men in each cellblock. He never searched my cell again. I guess he knew he was wrong and I think he may have gotten into trouble for what he did if the proper authorities knew. He is allowed to go through my legal papers but he can't throw them around the cell.

A couple of days later, we were coming back from chow and I tripped on what I thought was the doorstop while walking through the door. My friend Ginny and I were walking in together and now we were halfway down the first set of cells when this big guy who is behind me says, "Hey, man, you kicked my foot." "Oh, sorry about that pal," I replied and with this he throws a right hand punch to my eye. I didn't go down but I slid back a few feet. This guy figured he's going to make a reputation beating this small guy. My eye was purple in seconds. I came back with a series of blows to his stomach. I was throwing lefts and rights and giving it all I had but I just couldn't move this guy, he was so big and so strong. I was going to his stomach because I couldn't reach his face. The whistle started to blow and the hack was running toward us and the fight stopped for a bit. I was standing by my friend Ginny's cell where it happened, protecting my eye from being seen by the hack because he would know it was me that was in the fight. He was looking around to see who was fighting. He found nothing and left the scene. Ginny handed me a pipe he had hidden under his mattress and I walked up to this monster and said, "You and me punk, let's go to the square." The square is the very end of the back of the cellblock. It's used to hold the mops, brooms and pails and, in times like this, you both climb over the fence and it's just you and him. I was scared, very scared. This guy had to be more than 6 feet, at least 210-220 pounds and I'm 5'6", 150 pounds. I was holding this pipe behind me thinking that if this monster gets this pipe from me I'm a dead man but you have to be tough, you can't back down. "Come on punk, let's go," I said. "No," he says. "I don't want any trouble." "You don't want trouble you big f--king dope, then you shouldn't have started with me." He turned and walked away. "You're a piece of dirt," I said and I walked the other way.

A few days later while walking to the mess hall, I was pulled out of line. "What happened to your eye?" the hack asked. "You been in a fight?" "No, I fell down playing handball in the back of the block and caught it on the table. It should heal soon, I hope. Looks bad, huh?" I replied. "O.K. Get back in line," he said. He probably figured I was lying but he knew that was all he was getting. Prisons are filled with violence; you never know when a fight will break out. They can start over anything- a small disagreement, an argument, and even a card game if your partner thinks you played a stupid hand and he's in a bad mood, guys finding out their wife or girlfriend is leaving them or cheating on them can lead to a fight. Anything, almost anything, can lead to war. Tension runs high in prisons, especially in overcrowded prisons like Rikers Island. You never know and always have to be ready to defend yourself. If you don't defend yourself, you become prey and soon can wind up as someone's bitch. I've seen so much violence that it sickens my stomach. I've seen people cut up with razor blades. I've seen heads opened up with pipes and I even saw a guy scalded with a bucket of boiling hot water.

Homosexuality isn't that prevalent in men's prisons but there are always a few "ladies" in each cellblock. My friends and me didn't partake in those activities, although there were others that did. I looked at it as though that was their business and they can do their time any way they wish. Once I saw this young white kid being taken off by four members of another race. I wanted to help this young kid but he was doing nothing to help himself and as I walked by one guy said, "Not your business, Rykoff." Well, it was my business but with this kid not helping himself, I wasn't going to be playing hero so I just kept walking. Nothing could be done to help this poor kid. I couldn't become a snitch and call the guard. If I had, I'd soon be in the same position, and as a convict I lived by the code myself. If I called four or five friends and a fight broke out between whites and blacks, that would have touched off a race riot and, besides, my friends would have said what I thought, that this kid is not doing anything to help himself. My hands were tied.

A few weeks later, the cell block clerk was getting ready for release and suggested that I try for his job. "Are you crazy?" I asked. "You want me to work up front with this hack after what happened a few weeks ago?" "Al," he said, "when you work for this guy he's good, he looks out for his guys. Trust me on this." So I trusted him and went to see Capt. Adler and applied for the clerk's job and got it. Now I was in the office working for this man who harassed me for so long, the one I had the argument with and he turned out to be O.K. When my laundry connection would come by with my pressed clothes and I wasn't up front, he would take the package for me and put it in my drawer. Extra clothes weren't allowed and you were supposed to get your clothes at the bathhouse once a week, not delivered to your cell block, pressed and starched. After a while, we started joking with one another but still he was a cop and I was a criminal. Once he asked me for some information and I told him, "Please don't ask me things like that. I'm not a snitch. If I were, I wouldn't be here." He never asked me anything like that again. He knew the code as well as I did. He realized that just because we joke doesn't mean we're friends or on the same side of the fence. He went home at night. I didn't.

Rikers Island, like all jails, is a very prejudiced place. Whites stay with whites, and blacks with blacks, and Latinos with Latinos and I had a system set up not to cause problems. Next to every black guy's name I put a little line. Next to a Latino name, I put a dot and nothing next to a white guy's name. This way, when a black guy came in, I put him in a cell with a black guy. When a Latino guy came in, I put him with a Latino guy and the same for whites. That way everyone was happy and everyone appreciated what I had done for their people. Every few months the guard in charge of my block, whose name I can't remember, would switch everyone around putting whites with blacks, Latinos with whites or blacks. Almost everyone was moved. Every time this would happen, everyone would come to see me in the office. "Rykoff, what's going on?" they would ask. "We know it's not you but what can be done?" "Don't worry. At lock-in, just move back to where you were; I got you covered." Well, you had to see what would happen. At lock-in, you had about three hundred men running around with all their stuff. Once the guard who had the block at night said to me, "What the hell is going on here, Rykoff?" "Don't worry sir. I got it under control," I said.

One good thing about that job is that working with the guards you get to know them and you can get away with a lot. The guards at night don't really care. They come in one night and you may not see them again for a few weeks. Only the day shift is assigned to a cellblock steady. When a good hack was on at night and I wanted to talk to someone in another block, I would ask the officer, "Say Mr. X, who has Six Block tonight?" "Officer J's in charge of Six Block." "Hey, Mr. X, do me a favor and let me get over to Six Block; I got to see a friend of mine. I'm sure Officer J. will let me talk to them" and, in most cases, I got to where I wanted to go.

For the most part, I hated authority figures. One day a race riot broke out in Five Block. These can become bloody messes and the institution knew this had to be stopped right away because it always spreads from one block to another. There was a lot of tension in the prison that night. Almost everyone was getting their weapons together, pulling them out of their hiding places or making new ones. Weapons come in small packages so they can be hidden. Some have toothbrushes filed down to a thin point at the end like a knife. There are some that have razor blades attached to the end of a toothbrush. Others have razor blades on matches. We used to have wooden matches the length of a razor blade. You take one match, put a blade on top of it, then another match on top of that with another blade. On top of that goes another match and razor blade and it's held together with thread wrapped around the match end. Can you imagine that going across your face? There were so many different types of weapons and today I'm sure the prison population is even more inventive than we were years ago.

The next morning, Warden Thomas sent for two whites, two blacks and two Latinos from each block. I was one of the 24 that were marched to his office that morning. We were seated and the warden read us the riot act. "This better not spread to the other cell blocks. I want you guys to go back and tell your people that we will win, even if we have to send in the militia. "You guys, yeah, what do you want?" he asked when I raised my hand. "It's Friday morning, warden. I have to go to Jewish services," I said to the warden. "Take him to services," he told the guard and I left the room and went to services. I didn't want to hear what he was about to say. As far as I was concerned, he had said enough. Once again I was defying authority, once again I was saying "to hell with you." In reality, what could I have done but relayed his message and there was enough of a message at that point to relay. Who would listen? If you're attacked, you respond in kind. That time the riots did not spread but I did hear of some very bad ones. You're lucky to walk away from it, if you can walk after it's over. Remember the riot squad. They come in with big bats and just start to swing. Who they hit or where they hit that person means nothing to them. Their only objective is to stop the riot and they do a very good job at that. Things got back to normal and I was back working in my office later that day.

I remember once this guy Frankie came in with his partner, an old guy named Max. The younger guy came up to me and asked if I could put him and his partner together in one cell. I said, "I don't have an empty cell in the place but I got your back covered." I put him in a cell with my friend Marvin, who I knew from the streets, and his partner in with this old time drug addict friend of mine who had been using drugs for fifty-two years. A few minutes later, a tier man came up to me with four packs of cigarettes. The tier man said to me, "This is from the guy you put in with your friend Marvin." After I finished my paperwork, I went walking up to Marvin's cell and I asked Frankie if he sent this to me. "Yeah," he said. I stuck my arm through the cell bars and threw the cigarettes at him. "You asked me for a favor and I did you a favor but I'm not a jail house peddler," I said. With this, my friend Marvin jumped off his bunk and said, "Al, calm down, this guy's a friend of mine. My brother works for him." Marvin was the peacemaker. When the cells were open and everyone came out for chow, Marvin called me to the side. "Are you crazy?" he said, "This guy is connected, he's Mafia. You don't start up with people like this." "I don't care who he is Marvin. He insulted me," I said. As it ends up, Marvin calmed the situation down and Frankie, Max and I became good friends and played against each other at the bridge table every night. Marvin and I against Frankie and the old guy Max. I understand that Frankie today is doing 100 years in federal prison for racketeering. What can I say about that?

I did learn something that day. I learned that I had a chip on my shoulder and that was foolish. I could have very easily walked to his cell, returned the cigarettes and told him it wasn't necessary. I think that was the start of me maturing, because before that I was a stupid guy that thought he had all the answers. Understand that this isn't school but you can learn a lot about yourself in a prison environment.

I was starting to get very tired of prison life. Day after day, week after week, month after month, the same routine. Up at 4:30 A.M. In the mess hall at 5 A.M. Back in your cell till 8 A.M. Back out of the cell till 3:30 P.M... Lock back in while they change shifts. Lock out at 4:15 P.M. Go to chow. Back to the cellblock until lock in at about 9 P.M. and lights out at 10 P.M. Working inside as block clerk gave me only one day a week to sit in the sun. Sunday, we would go to the yard during the summer months. During the winter, guys that work within the institution never see the sun.

One day, a few months later, I was playing bridge. We had those wooden picnic benches that hold eight people and there were two games going at once. Somebody cracked a joke. I don't remember the joke but I remember laughing. While I was laughing, I looked around the table and, although everyone was laughing, I didn't see anyone's eyes smiling. This startled me and a strange feeling came over me that evening. Later that night when lock-in was called, I went back to my cell and looked in the mirror. "What the hell am I doing here with these guys?" I thought. "These are hardened criminals. Who am I fooling? I'm not like them. I can't kill anyone; I'm not a big thief." I kept thinking. Mostly I sold drugs or stole something small, and I never really liked stealing. I washed up, got into bed and thought, "What's become of my life? Where is it going? Will I ever get married, have children, work and live a normal life?" We think we're so hip and refer to people who don't use drugs as squares but think about those squares. They're out there with their girlfriends, holding hands, having dinner, dancing, and here I am in this little cell, alone with more than six thousand other inmates all around me that have no idea who they really are. One thing about jail is that inmates are all images. They show toughness but it's when they're in the cell at night and thinking that most know it's all an act, an image. Has my life since I'm a young kid been a lie, a lie so strong that it fooled me? Is this always going to be my life or is it time I stood up and changed? I got up, looked in the mirror again and went to sleep knowing that it was now time to get it together.

CHAPTER TWO
THE BATTLE BEGINS

THE NEXT DAY MY brother came to visit me. He now was returning the favor I did for him years before by smuggling drugs to me. "Bring anything?" I asked. "No, not this time," he replied. "Good," I said. "Don't bring it any more. I'm not getting high again. It's over. I don't want to see it, smell it or touch it, I'm finished." He, of course, couldn't understand this. How could a drug addict turn down drugs, especially in jail, but he did grant my wish. In fact, he was happy I made that decision. That night I wrote the Executive Director of Daytop a letter explaining that I realize I need help and know that I have to get it together before it's too late. I told him that when I'm released I wanted to return to the program and get my life in order. In days, I got a reply explaining that he's happy I realize where my problems lie, and although he won't say "Welcome back," he will grant me an interview.

Well, an interview was all I needed. I knew enough about Daytop to know that if you're sincere about getting some help, you will be accepted. At the time, I still had no idea as to when I would be released. I still hadn't heard from the parole board. I was expecting to do at least the better part of the three years because I had left Daytop, so my mind was ready for that. From that day forward, I started to think more positively.

I didn't tell any of my friends about my decision. Number one, it was nobody's business where I go or what I do after my release and, number two, I was maintaining my image. I was the guy bringing the drugs in the cellblock so there was nothing I had to turn down from anyone else. Once in a while, a good friend who I shared my drugs with would ask if I was getting anything and I just said, "No, but if it happens, I got you covered." Life went on as usual, working in my office up front and playing bridge in my spare time.

One day in the yard, I was sitting by myself. I didn't feel like hanging out with my friends. I just wanted to be alone and think, take in the sun and relax. A friend of mine that had just come through the reception center told me that my brother was there with a one-year sentence. "He got here yesterday," I was told. I couldn't understand how I wasn't informed earlier about his arrest, only to find out he got arrested one day, sentenced the next and sent to Rikers Island on the third day. I was preparing for his arrival because I was clerk of the receiving block and he had to come through me. I waited for a cell to open and held it open for him so that he could "lock" alone; in other words, have his own cell. Living two in a cell is not easy because the cells are small and although this is prison life, if you can get around it, you do. At the same time, I didn't want him in with me. The clerk gets his own cell and I liked it that way. Messages known to us as "kites" were going back and forth. Soon I found out they were keeping him in the reception center because they didn't want to put us together for security reasons. Damn, I was mad and pleaded my case to captain Warfield but my request to have my brother sent from the reception center to the penitentiary was denied. Messages kept going back and forth. New guys coming from the reception center would bring news every day and guys going to the reception center for their release would give him word about me. This is all we had. Here was my brother, my role model, my mentor, on the same island and we could not see or talk to each other.

One day, about two weeks later, I was summoned to the Deputy Warden's office. "What's this all about?" I wondered, as I was being escorted. Thoughts went through my mind. "Is my mom all right? Is my brother all right?" As we arrived at the office, the door was opened and sitting in front of me was my brother. "I arranged this with Social Services," he said. My brother had arranged visits once a week for an hour in the Deputy

Warden's office. The visits were on a Saturday and the Deputy was not at work then. I always felt the room was bugged but I'll never know. In those days I trusted nobody. We talked and I explained my plans. "I'm going back to Daytop the day I'm released," I said. "I'm finished using. I've had nine years of this life and I'm tired of it." My brother was happy that I made that decision. Living that life is bad enough, but having your kid brother live it is even harder and although most of my life patterns were due to my brother raising me the way he did, he really did love me and I knew he felt guilty about my using for a long time. He was very happy about my decisions to go back to Daytop but I was unable to talk him into coming with me. I had time, though. We still had eight months left on our sentences.

A few weeks later I got word from the Parole Board. I would have to serve fourteen months of my three-year sentence. "Not bad," I thought. I was expecting much more. In thinking about it, I realized Daytop is an 18-month program and I had spent four months there. This was the remaining 14 months. I guess that was the Parole Board's way of saying, "You idiot, you're off the streets anyway, but had you stayed in Daytop, you could have gotten it together." At that time, I also had eight months left. My release date was for one Tuesday in August 1966. Parole cases only get out on Tuesdays but I didn't know which Tuesday. Weeks turned into months and time was going by. The visits with my brother were still coming, and, on each visit, I would ask my brother to come to Daytop when he got out. I was relentless, I never stopped asking him. His answer was always the same. "I'll see," his way of saying no. As my release date got closer, I went to pre-parole, a meeting with your parole officer to map out your program. This takes place about four months before your release. He wanted to know where I would live and where I would work. "I'm going to live at 450 Bayview Ave, Staten Island," I said. "Staten Island," he said. "Your family is from Brooklyn. Why are you going to Staten Island?" "I'm going to a place called Daytop Village." Daytop had changed their name from Daytop Lodge to Daytop Village and was now accepting females. I explained that Daytop was a rehabilitation center. "A rehabilitation center," he said. "Aren't you rehabilitated now?" Well, a 3-year indefinite sentence on Rikers Island is considered a rehabilitation sentence, and if I tell this guy I'm not rehabilitated, I don't get out so I said, "I'm rehabilitated in terms of drugs, but I want to further my rehabilitation in terms of being a man." "I can't accept that as your program," he said. "Why not?" I asked. "There is no guarantee that you will be accepted into this program," he added. "I have this letter here from the Executive Director granting me an interview," I said. "All I need to get in this program is to show them that I'm sincere and who can be more sincere than I am after spending 14 months in here? I'm not going into the streets; I'm going to Daytop." "No," he said. "You can't go there."

Soon, I started to argue with this guy until I realized I can't argue with him. He holds the key to my freedom and to continue to argue would be foolish on my part. I said, "O.K. sir. I'll live with my mother in Brooklyn and work for my uncle at Nemar Products, where they make parts for lamps." Soon the interview was over and I went back to my cell block. I was mad and I was pacing. Up and down, up and down. I don't know how many times I walked up and down the cell block that day but all I knew was I had to find a way to get back to Daytop. I knew if I went back into the streets, I would use drugs. Even if I didn't want to, I would end up using.

I paced till lock-in at which time I went back into my cell and wrote Daytop a letter again. I explained almost word for word what took place earlier that day while talking to the parole officer and I told them that since the Parole Department wouldn't let me go to the program, that what I intended to do was turn down parole and take the City of New York to court for stopping me from further rehabilitation. I knew then that this would take another year at the least to have this case heard in court and maybe they would keep postponing it until I finished the three years but there was no way I was going into the streets before I knew I was ready to go into the streets. Well, when David, the Executive Director, saw this letter he knew I was sincere and he went to the Parole Department and spoke on my behalf. Three days later, I got a letter from David saying, "Congratulations, Allan, you are now a member of the Daytop family. You will be released to us and finish your parole under our roof." These were the words I wanted to hear. This was the biggest battle in my life so far, and one that I had to win. I knew then I was on my way to a better life, a normal life. I knew I had to find out who Allan was, what made Allan tick and why I was living the life I had lived. I was, as they say, a happy camper.

My brother had a friend who worked in the Records Room check my folder and found out that we had the same release date. He sent me a kite letting me know our release date was August 16th, 1966. It was like a miracle. I was doing 14 months of a three year sentence and he was doing eight months of a one-year sentence and we were both getting out on the same day. I thought maybe it's for a reason; maybe I can get my brother to come with me. I now had about four months left. Soon, I broke the hundreds, the term used for having less than a hundred days left. I was "getting short" as we say in jail. The days were getting longer the closer I got to my release date. I was still asking my brother to come with me. "Hey, we're getting out on the same day. Let's go together," I would tell him. "I'll see, I'll see." That was the answer I got every time I mentioned it.

The days kept getting longer and longer. There are twenty-four hours in a day for most people but not for the people getting out of prison. For them, the days have forty hours. I had gotten out of prison so many times before, but this time it wasn't the same. This time I really wanted it, this time my mouth was watering. This time it was a rebirth.

On my job, one of my responsibilities as block clerk was to get on the P.A. system at night after everyone was locked in and call out the hold-in's for the next day. People are held in for a number of reasons: clinic appointments, social service appointments, work assignment appointments, hospital appointments, attorney appointments and a variety of others. In the morning, after chow when everyone was back in their cells, I would call them again. I would always call the name and the number of the inmate and tell them what the hold-in was for. "Jones 555-5555 social service" and I would go down the list calling everyone that had a hold-in. When the officer comes in the block to pick up their hold-ins, I would get on the speaker again. All social service hold-ins up front. One day a guy didn't come up front for his appointment. "Call him again," I was told by the officer picking up his hold-ins. So I did and still he didn't show up. Then the guard asked me to go up and down the cellblock calling his name and I said, "Sir, I called this guy last night, again this morning and you just heard me call it again. What more can I do?" "You can run up and down the block calling his name," he said. "I'm not running up and down no cellblock. That's why I have a P.A. system in my office." "Are you refusing a direct order from me?" he replied. "Not exactly," I said. "I just don't think there's a need for it. The guy ain't deaf."

"Face the wall," he told me. The guard who ran my block was somewhere in the back. I knew he would get me out of this but I couldn't get to him. I wanted to get on the P.A. system and call for him saying "come up front. I got a problem here" but when an officer tells you to get up against the wall, you don't move. The guard locked me up for insubordination and I found myself in solitary confinement. Solitary is in the basement under Cellblock One. You're in a strip cell. Just you, no toothbrush, toothpaste or soap, no mattress or pillow, no toilet paper, cigarettes, books or anything. At night they give you a few blankets and that's it. When you have to go to the bathroom you have to first hold your arm through the bars and ask for the toilet paper. "Toilet paper in fourteen," I would yell. It's cold and damp down there during the winter months and hot and sticky during the summer months. You're fed one meal every three days. For the other meals, you get four slices of bread and whatever they're having to drink at that meal, coffee, tea or milk. Today it's not like that. Today inmates have constitutional rights and are fed all their meals.

I spent a week there and then went up to see Captain Adler for reassignment. "Where do you want to work?" he asked and I said, "I want my job back as the clerk of Two Block." "No," he said. "That's one of the better jobs in the institution and I have to save it for a guy that's going to be here for a while. You're short, you got one foot out the door. I do want you to know that the officer in charge of Two Block came to me and asked to get you back," he said, "You're a good guy and a hard worker." That officer, the one that harassed me for so long, the one I had that argument with, turned out to be one of the best guards in the place. "Well, Capt. Adler, why don't you just let me lay up and not assign me to any job?" and he said, "O.K." This way I was able to play bridge all day and pass the time that way.

The days were getting longer now. I didn't realize till then how much the job helped me get through those days. How many card games can you play in one day? How many hours can you sit on those wooden benches? This time, for the first time ever, I had something to look forward to when I got out. For the first time, I had a new beginning, a fresh start, a new life, and how bad I wanted to start that new life. I knew my life would change and I knew the prospect of using drugs, going in and out of prison and possibly dying at a young age were gone. I knew I would never have to look back. I would just look forward to a great life. The days were dragging and with thirty days left I started counting. Each night, I would wait for lights out knowing that when I woke up I can cross another day off the calendar. I started counting the meals also and what made me laugh was walking into the mess hall and finding a meal that I didn't like and wouldn't eat. "Didn't need to count this one," I would tell myself. With one week left, I was transferred to the Reception Center for release. "It was true," I thought. "I got one foot out the door and another one on a banana peel," as the saying goes.

I would see my brother in the hall on the way to chow. He'd be coming out of the mess hall as I was going in and we would nod to one another, as there is no talking in the halls. In the yard on that last weekend, I still insisted he come with me, but now his answer was, "No, not right away. I'll meet you there." "This ain't no country club," I said. "You just don't meet people there and come and go as you please. I can get you in now but you have to come with me Tuesday." "No," he told me. "Not right now." I knew what he wanted; he wanted to get high. You don't have to be a college graduate to figure that one out. I knew it and he knew it, but he wasn't honest enough to admit it.

Tuesday came and my brother and I were in a cell called the Bullpen, a large cell used to hold guys getting released. There were about 30 guys in with us. Again I asked him to come with me and again he said, "No." We started to argue. I knew it was my last chance to convince him to come to Daytop. We argued so much that one guy we knew came up to us and said, "You guys better cool it, you'll never get out if you keep this up." He went to one end of the cell and I stayed on the other. When they called his name for release he walked over to me, shook my hand and said, "Take care. I'll see you in a few days." I didn't know it then, but that would be the last time I would ever see my brother or talk to him again.

My name was called a while later and I, along with some other guys, was taken by bus to the Parole Department in New York City. The ride was long but nice. Looking at people, seeing kids play in the street, it was beautiful. We arrived at the Parole Board. "Sit down," the parole officer said. "You know the routine." Well, I didn't know the routine; this was my first time going out on parole. He had got me mixed up with my brother but I was in no mood to argue. I just wanted to get to Daytop. After a while, he released me.

I first went to where my mother worked at the Gund Manufacturing Company to say hello. When I saw her, I gave her a big hug and a kiss and we walked off to talk. As we were walking, she said to me, "Allan, do whatever they tell you to do. If Daytop tells you to stand on your head, then stand on your head." "Don't worry, mom, someday you're going to be very proud of me." "I hope so," she said. I gave her another hug and then it was off to Daytop.

My mother lived a tough life. My father passed away when she was in her thirties, leaving her with two small children. She worked hard to see that we had what we needed, but the thing we needed most, discipline, she couldn't give us. She wasn't a strong woman. Hard worker in the office she worked in, good cook, kept the house spotless, was a very sweet honest lady, but could not control her sons. What she went through with two addicted sons was awful. When we were on Rikers Island at the same time, it was especially hard for her. First, she had to wake up early, walk about a mile to the train station and take the train from Brooklyn to the Bronx, about 2 ½ hours. Then, a bus to the ferry. She would register and come over to the island to see one of us. Our visits were an hour every two weeks. We would see each other through a glass window and talk on a phone. After visiting one of us, she then had to take the ferry back to the mainland, re-register and then take the ferry over again to see the other son. Then, of course, the train ride back to Brooklyn and the walk home again. She never missed a visit. In all those years, between my brother and myself, we spent 17 years in prison. My mother never missed a visit. Well, as far as I was concerned, she would never see me in jail again.

I first took the train to Brooklyn to get the bus to cross the bridge into Staten Island. On the train, I was thinking of all the years in jail and some of the funny things that happened to me, like the time in 1961 when I worked in the mess hall. My job was giving out the bread, four slices to each inmate. Before lunch, my friends Skeeter, Red and I were just sitting around talking when Red said something about my being Jewish. Well, you just don't let people get away with something like talking bad about your religion. I said, "Come on you f-king bum, I'm going to break your ass." Red and I went into a small room while Skeeter stood by the door watching for the hack. Red and I were battling. It was a good hard-fought fight that I won. I walked out of the room and told Skeeter to get inside and help Red and I went to the bathroom to wash up. That, in itself, is not funny but what made it funny was when all the cell blocks came in for chow. As the cellblocks would enter the mess hall, there were two lines in. All the guys would be on my line for two reasons. Number one, they were my friends and would always say "hello," plus I was the passer. I would move things from block to block. Someone in Two Block would give me something for someone in Three Block, someone from Four Block would send something to Seven Block and I would pass the packages to whoever it was for. The funny part of the story was when Two Block came in, the guys said that they heard me and Red had it out. "Yeah, it's over," I said. Three Block came in. "Heard you blackened his eye." "No man, he's O.K.," I said. Four Block, "Hey, heard you broke his nose." "No man, he's O.K." Five Block, "We hear Red's all busted up." "No, he's O.K.," I would say. Six Block, Seven Block and by Eight Block, Red was almost dead. Thank God, we didn't have a Nine Block because by then the word would have been that I killed him.

I had switched jobs that year and went to work on landscaping. Landscaping was a good job and we would maintain the grassy areas. We would always find a way to sneak over to the chicken farm to get some eggs, then go back and cook them. Much better than powdered eggs. I remember the landscaping boss (the guard), who liked to be called "Boss." One day he had an idea to cause us some problems. We had two trees that were so big, so fat around, that I thought the roots would be down so far they were touching China.

One day, the boss told me, "Get your gang together and pull those two trees out of the ground." "Boss," I said, "I don't have a gang. If you mean my friends, none of them will be here ten years from now because that's how long it will take for these trees to be removed." "You heard me, pull those trees out." Well, me and four guys walked over to these trees with shovels, looked at the trees, threw our shovels on the ground and just lay down and lit up a cigarette. There was no way we could get these trees out of the ground. As we're laying back relaxing, here comes a construction worker in a big machine which name escapes my memory right now, one with wheels like a tank with a big scoop in front of it. The construction workers were there building a women's prison on the island, we heard. One of my friends walks up to this guy and says, "Think you can pull these trees out of the ground for us?" "Sure, no problem." So he ties a large chain around the first tree, puts his machine in reverse and pulls this giant tree out. "How about the second one?" we say. "Sure, no problem." So he pulls the second one out without a problem. Later, we're sitting back relaxing and the boss comes by. Well, you had to see the look on his face. This was nothing but an harassment job that he gave us. Now the trees were out and lying on the ground. The boss walked by and couldn't believe his eyes. "How'd you do this?" he said. "Boss, you wanted the trees out, they're out and we worked our ass off to get them out for you, so now you're going to question it?" He walked away scratching his head and we stayed behind to relax. Well, I guess you had to be there for that one, but it was the look on his face that made it so funny.

I thought about a lot of friends I had in prison and thought about them spending year after year in places like that. I thought about some real funny guys who would keep us laughing all night long and there were plenty of them. I had a friend who was deaf and mute and he was the funniest one I ever met in prison. He had a way of communicating a story that you knew just what he was saying and what funny stories he had to tell.

The train came to my stop and I took the bus over the bridge.

Well, here I was again on a bus crossing the Verrazano Bridge into Staten Island. This time, it was not the same as the last time. This time, I was going there because I wanted to be there, not just to get away from a jail sentence. This time, I had a purpose, I had hope and I had visions of a great life. This time, I was determined. I had dreams. I had waited for this day for a long time and now it was here and I knew I had to make the best of this. I knew I had to stop fighting the system and that I had to let Daytop in. I was bracing for the biggest battle of my life, but it wasn't going to be a fight. It was going to be won with determination, with hard work and with openness. Daytop can be harder than jail. Here, all the responsibility is on you. In jail, you have almost no responsibility. They wake you up in the morning. They tell you when to eat and what to eat. They put you back into your cells. They let you out of those cells. You go to work and they tell you what to do. They tell you when it's time to eat breakfast, lunch and dinner, when to lock in and when to lock out. They even put the lights on and off for you. All you have to do is follow directions. In Daytop or any therapeutic community, you are the one responsible for everything you do and that can make it harder for people like us who weren't very responsible.

I crossed the bridge and got on the bus to Tottenville and, this time, the trip evoked other thoughts. If you didn't know it, Staten Island has lots of beautiful women and it had been so long since I was able to even look at a woman. This, I knew, had to be set aside. First things first and getting my life in order was top priority and there was nothing more important than that. I knew that every dog gets his chance to bark and one day I to will be able to bark real loud.

I got off at Bayview Ave. I'm now walking up that dirt road leading to the house on the hill. That house on the hill. How bad I wanted to get there and get started. To see all the guys that were there the first time I was in Daytop. I walked in and was greeted by an old friend and then told to sit down on the chair once again but this time it wasn't the same. Some guys that had been with me the first time were coming over and saying hello. Now they weren't just residents, they were staff, directors, assistant directors and coordinators. They were all doing well except for me, the guy that thought he had all the answers. What a fool I was. Had I stayed there, I could have been feeling good about myself by now but it was too late to cry over spilled milk and I realized that today will be the start of my comeback.

Within minutes, I was taken to the director's office and I knew everyone there. This time there was no ridiculing interview. I was asked how I felt and I answered, "Fine, glad to be back." The interview took no more then two minutes after sharing hellos. Then they told me they wanted me to address the house, the entire population, and explain my story to them and I knew that I was the tool to help others who think they were smarter than the program and maybe thinking of leaving. A house meeting was called and everyone gathered in one large room. I was introduced and told my story. I explained how I thought I had all the answers, how I thought I could leave, use drugs and not get caught. I explained that I was out only 32 days and got three years, serving 14 months of that sentence. I went on to talk about the joke told during the card game and how I looked around and saw no one's eyes smiling and how it affected me. I talked about why I came back and how I intend to get my life in order. I talked about living a good life starting today. I talked about the hopes and dreams I had for the future. As I finished, the facility director who was standing in the back of the room said, "Welcome back, Al."

I was in the door. After all that emotional stress which included that conversation with my parole officer, contemplating turning down parole and not being allowed to do what I knew I needed to save my life, here I was back in Daytop. It wasn't going to be easy. Learning about yourself and talking about yourself in front of others never is, but I wanted to change, I had to change, and I knew my life was at stake. Three days after entering Daytop, I was transferred to the Swan Lake facility in the Catskills. What a beautiful place that was on 129 acres, if I remember correctly, a main house with two large buildings on each end with a few bungalows and a large lake. At one time, this was the Paul's Hotel.

The day after I arrived in Swan Lake, I was summoned to the director's office. I walked in and the director told me he has some bad news for me. I knew right away it was my brother but out of respect I said, "My mother?" "No," he replied. "My brother?" I asked. "Yes," he said. "He's dead?" "Yes," was his reply. "Overdose?" I asked. "Yes" was the answer. I got up to walk out of the office and he asked, "Want to talk about it?" "No," I said and I walked out.

Seminar was going on and I broke into it. I thought this is the one chance my brother, who screwed up his life, who screwed up my life, would now have to help one hundred and fifty people in one shot. I got permission and broke into seminar. I explained to everyone that I was called into the office and told that my brother had died. "I'd like to tell you all about my brother. He was 32 years old, one of the smartest people you could ever meet, but who used those smarts in a negative way. He had spent about 12 years in prison. He was never married and had no children and now he's dead of an overdose and that's what happens to drug addicts. You play and you pay, only the payment cost more than the playing and you wind up the loser. In reality, we're all losers. That's why we're here, to learn how to become winners, and I suggest that we learn our lessons well. Otherwise, we can all end up like my brother."

With this, I walked out of the room and got permission to call my mother. I couldn't reach her. She wasn't at home where I thought she would be, so I called her office figuring that she went to work trying to forget. Her office told me she was at my Aunt Laura's house on Long Island, so I called there. After I spoke to my aunt, my mother got on the phone. This conversation I really can't remember, although I do recall her saying, "He's happy now. He was buried like a general." "Was this supposed to make me feel better?" I thought. She was still talking but I was too stunned to hear anything, although I remember her last words to me. She said, "Allan, please don't do anything to hurt me now." What she meant was, don't leave the program. No, I wasn't leaving the program. My right arm was just torn away from me. Now, I really had no reason to leave. No reservations at all. I spent the next few days down by the lake by myself, just thinking. How many times did I ask him to come with me? Week after week I asked, the day of our release I asked, and I was sure that our release date being the same was done for a reason. God was giving him one last chance to make the right decision. He didn't. I always felt my father had arranged that. I asked but all I got was "I'll see." Three days he lasted, three days out of jail and he was dead of an overdose. It's true what I said to the house; that's what happens to drug addicts. You either spend your life in and out of prison or you die. I was lucky, I found a way out only now, and I had to make this work for me. For the first time in my life, I had no one to depend on. For the first time in my life, I was totally alone and I knew I had to grow up fast. I now felt what I was told in my first interview. I was a twenty-six year old baby.

After a few days of moping around, I started to get back into the swing of things, participating in everything, morning meetings, seminars, group encounters and marathon sessions. Group encounters were still hard for me. Opening yourself up for all to see is not easy. Talking about your fears, your inadequacies and your shortcomings is hard but necessary to learn about yourself. Until we see ourselves we can never change ourselves. Talking about yourself is like taking all those bad feelings that you had bottled up for so long out of your belly and placing them on a table to examine them. It makes it that much easier to see and then to change. You also have the support of the entire group helping you first to pull it out, then to see it better. No matter who they are, white, black or brown, everyone was there to help everyone. Now it's time to find away to deal with those feelings and change those feelings. Once that takes place, you start to feel a little better about yourself. Slowly over time, change is created.

Soon, I started to move up the ladder. First, I started to write the house newspaper, and every morning I would read it to the house during the morning meeting. I always tried to put some funny things in it to get people started with a smile on their face. I was working in the kitchen when my brother died. I can't cook for the life of me, yet I was told by some that I was the best cook Daytop had. Go figure. Soon I became the switchboard operator. We had one of those old systems where you plug the cord into the hole. "One moment please, I will connect you". After that, I became an expediter and was doing rather well.

I was one of the few people in the house who had a driver's license so I became the house driver as well. I would be the one going back and forth to the Staten Island facility rotating people and supplies. I would also drive deserving people to the movies and pick them up again when the show ended. I would drive people to doctors' offices and much, much more. One day, while driving back to the facility with some people in the car on a very cold winter night, it was snowing very hard and the roads were filled with snow and ice and it became hard to see. I must have hit an ice patch. The car went out of control and I hit a tree. I knew then that I was in trouble. We got back to the house and I was called to the Director's office and given a "haircut." A haircut is a verbal reprimand. I was striped of all my responsibilities and my head was shaved. I was given a sign to wear, saying I was irresponsible and that I needed help. I was at the bottom of the ladder. Not a good feeling but one that I had to learn to deal with. A kid walking in the door had more status than me but I didn't let it throw me. I was determined to move right back up again. I was talking to the Executive Director one day and I said, "I was just doing 10 miles an hour," and his answer to me was, "Well, Al, I guess you should have been doing 5 miles an hour." You can't win. Reality is, I did damage a Daytop vehicle and that, as the driver, was my responsibility. My concern now wasn't the car. Yes, I felt bad about it but the fact is, it's only a piece of metal. My concern centered on finding a way to deal with being the dingbat of the facility, the low man on the totem pole.

I started to take on more responsibility on my own, helping out here and helping out there. We call that seeking and assuming responsibility. I would go to every department asking if I could help with something when I had some free time, "What can I do to help you people?" I would ask. I continued using all the tools of the program and I was starting to be noticed. Al was not sitting on his butt, Al was fighting back and doing it the right way, with hard work and determination and Al was being noticed. Everyone knew, there was no stopping me now.

About a month later, I was called to the Director's office and he said, "We need someone to run the Supply Department. Think you can handle it?" "A piece of cake," I said. I was put in charge of the Supply Department and had the title of Department Head. I was moving up. I started to joke about it because I was the only one in the department. I would tell my friends, "I'm the only department head here that has no department. I'm the boss and I'm the worker" and we would laugh but I did my job well. I was responsible for all donations coming into the facility, mostly clothing. I would size them, label them and hang them up. When people needed clothes, they came to me. I would give them what they needed and keep a running inventory. Soon, I became a group leader running group encounter sessions on Monday, Wednesday and Friday evenings. Me, who at one time was so afraid of these sessions because you were open for all to see, was now the group leader helping others to open up.

Soon I was celebrating my one-year birthday in Daytop, the year 1967. My mother had sent me a beautiful star sapphire ring, which I still wear to this day. At this point I still hadn't seen my mother since the day I was released from prison.

Soon after that, an announcement was made in morning meeting. Daytop, with the help of an off- Broadway director, was starting a drama group. I thought "this can be fun" and I remembered back to the days in the sixth grade when I could and should have gotten the lead in "Ali-Baba and The Forty Thieves." I also thought it would be easy, I'm a ham anyway. I'll read some lines and perform. How hard can that be so I raised my hand and became a member of the drama group. "Easy," I thought. It was far from easy.

We had a large theater, that wasn't being used, on the property from when it used to be a hotel. Now there was a use for this building. We would start by doing some exercises on the floor every morning. Then, as a group, we would do humming exercises to put us in sync with one another. There were also no plays to read. We had to write our own play. Here we were, eight ex-addicts who had never acted, most never even seeing a play and we had to write and perform our own. As months went by, we put together a play called "The Concept." The maintenance crew built us a stage and we performed it for all at the Swan Lake facility and everyone loved it. I couldn't understand why we didn't use the theater to perform the play, only to find out from the director that he wanted this play to be done with the audience on three sides. Soon, we heard that the Staten Island facility was building a stage and we put the play on over there. They loved it as well. We then found ourselves doing it at Seton Hall University and they loved it also. Soon, we got news that we were headed for what's known as Off, Off Broadway in New York City. We did it every night for a week. The reviews were great and we were full of joy. A few weeks later we were called back to Off, Off Broadway for a repeat performance and again it was good.

Once my mother, my Aunt Bobby, Uncle Sid and Cousin Jeffrey came to see us perform. I remember that, while I was speaking, I heard my aunt tell my mother, "Mary, he doesn't even know we're here." Well, I knew they were there, only I was afraid to look at them for fear I might start to cry because I became so emotional about this play, and about what I, along with other members of the drama group, had accomplished and because I knew how proud my mother was of me. That always touched me. (This was the first time I had saw my mother since being in Daytop.) We had a great play and we performed it just as good. We always ended to a standing ovation, always. Since we performed it on a stage that had people on three sides, when we took our bows, four of us would go to one side and the other four would be on the other side. We took two bows and would switch sides for two bows, finally meeting in the center. All the time people were on their feet cheering. Then we would walk off stage and be called back again. It was always the same way. I remember the first time we did the play and came out for a curtain call. I said to myself, "Wow, they're still standing." I was so proud of this play that I kept the script for about ten years till one day someone from Daytop called me asking if I still had it because Daytop wanted to do it again. I knew just where the script was and sent it to them. I hope they were as successful as we were.

I continued getting myself together, learning more each day about myself and about others. I was learning how to deal with situations and with people and I was feeling pretty good about myself. Life started to take on a new meaning for me. For the first time in my life, I was feeling good about Allan. Confident about Allan.

After the drama group had ended, I was given one of the highest and most reasonable jobs in Daytop, that of the Guru (the wise man). I was responsible for setting up all the group encounter sessions and marathon sessions, which were groups lasting 36 plus hours. You don't leave the room, food is brought in and there is no sleeping. These groups are designed to break down peoples' defenses in an effort to get them to talk about the worst thing they ever did in their life, the one thing that has them feeling so bad about themselves that they destroy their life by using drugs. Addiction takes on other avenues as well. Alcohol is one we're all aware of, but then there is the work alcoholic and what about the guy that spends 18 hours a day thinking and doing the same thing day after day? He may or may not have the same problems the addict has, but, if he does, he just found a more constructive way of dealing with them.

As Guru, I had no bosses. I reported right to the Assistant Director. One of my responsibilities was talking to people who wanted to leave the program and, I'm proud to say, that once they spoke to me they all decided to stay. Not that many people wanted to leave, but for those that did, once I spoke to them they all changed their minds and I never lost anyone while I held that position.

I had spent 14 months in prison and now I was in Daytop for over a year and was feeling the need for the opposite sex. Swan Lake was a small town at that time, with only a post office and about 4 small stores. It had one police officer, an older guy named Jack, who would always wave when we drove down the road. During the summer months, there were lots of people in the Catskills, which, at that time, was a summer resort area. During the winter months, there were but a handful of people. It has since changed, I understand, and the Catskills with its mountains and as much snow as they get has become a winter resort area as well.

With this new need of mine, I thought about getting rotated to the Staten Island facility, a decision that was hard to make. I had grown up in Swan Lake, changed my entire life there. My attitude was gone, my way of thinking was better, and I learned how to deal with inadequacies, fears and disappointment. I had a good sense of morals and values. I learned to communicate like an adult. I learned to care, to share and to love. This was now my home. I had lots of status, and there was lots of room with its 129 acres. How would life change if I got rotated? I knew nothing about me would change. The individual was strong, that wasn't going to be a problem, but although Staten Island was a large house it was about a tenth of the size of Swan Lake. I loved the room we had upstate with the lake and I never did mention the Olympic-sized swimming pool. Because Staten Island was smaller, it was a faster-paced house. Did I want that? Could I be happy there? Daytop is one large family and I knew everyone in each facility. Chain letters were sent back and forth regularly and you had a chance to communicate with your friends. I had spent time there because I was the house driver and would be the person bringing people back and forth. I would drive people down, sleep there and drive back the next day about once or twice a month but spending a night there is not like living there.

Finally, after about a month, I made my decision and walked into the director's office and announced that I wanted to be rotated to Staten Island. "Why? What's up, Al?" I was asked. "Well, Ed, I have some needs that Daytop can't help me with, the need for a woman, to share feelings that cannot be shared in a place where all the women are my sisters. I need a special kind of companionship. I need to love and to be loved. I need affection and I need to give affection and Swan Lake doesn't offer me the opportunity for that situation, Staten Island does."

Both facilities had Open House every Saturday night. Swan Lake would get about ten people, some coming every Saturday. We called them the regulars. Nice people who became very friendly with all of us. It was always nice to see them on Open House night and, I guess, for them, it was nice also because that area at the time didn't offer much to do on Saturday evenings. Staten Island on Saturday night would draw crowds of around 50 to 60 people and very few regulars. Meeting someone there was a shot in the dark and I'm not a gambler, but I had dreams.

I remembered the dream that brought me to Daytop in the first place. I had followed that dream and found myself. Now, maybe if I follow this dream, I'll find something else that I need. "Think you're going to find someone at open house?" The director asked. "There's a shot, Ed, but as long as I've been around, maybe I could get permission to go to a dance or maybe find another way, anyway, but here in this facility it's just about impossible." Three days later, with my bags packed, I was headed for Staten Island. I don't remember where I worked when I got to Staten Island, but I'm sure it was a job of responsibility. In Staten Island, I wasn't meeting anyone from the opposite sex that I was able to date but I was still into the program and that was my number one concern. I continued on, but at this point I was mostly helping others; taking new people under my wing and teaching them how to fly was such a great feeling for me. Running them data also reinforces it in us and I did that everyday but something was missing in me, something I needed and wanted.

Soon my thoughts changed and I started to think of the future. How nice it would be if I had a girlfriend, a job, a little car and an apartment. I knew I was ready. I felt very confident that if I left Daytop, I could go into society and live a normal life like everyone else. A few more months went by and my parole was over and I kept thinking about leaving. "I can do it," I kept saying. "I'm ready, I'm ready." I was having sleepless nights thinking about this. Could I just walk away, give up my friends who were now my family? Daytop didn't think I was ready to graduate; I did. My mind was going back and forth. One day I was thinking about staying. The next day I was thinking about leaving. I was torn between them both. One day while relaxing in my room I thought, I came here on a dream and fulfilled my mission, now I have other dreams to be fulfilled. I want to work, to live on my own, to be independent, to help my mother, to meet a woman, and maybe start a family. I thought and thought and thought until one morning I got up early, packed my bags and walked out the door. I had left Daytop.

On the bus ride back to Brooklyn, I wasn't so confident. I kept thinking, "Damn, I got a police record as long as my arm. Who the hell is going to hire me?" but I was on my way and I had to at least try. I got to Brooklyn and it felt strange being there. I walked up the stairs to my mother's house. It had been almost three years since I had been home. To my delight, everything was the same. My mother was surprised to see me. "What happened?" she asked. "Relax, ma, don't worry, I'll be fine," I replied. "What are you going to do?" she asked me. "I'll get the paper Sunday and go looking for a job early Monday morning," I said with confidence. She said she was talking to Freddy's mother (Freddy being the guy from my first interview in Daytop that told the director I'd be a tough cookie) and he started a program in Westchester County. My mother gave me the number and I called Freddy. The conversation lasted two minutes. "You dressed?" he asked. "Yeah," I replied. "I'll pick you up in a few minutes. Tell your mother not to worry, you have a job," That was easy, I thought.

Freddy came over with my friend Tom who I had known from Daytop. Hellos were exchanged and the three of us left. The ride was beautiful. I felt so free, so relaxed, so good. My mother must have been very nervous that day, but I was fine. We went to their office in City Hall, New Rochelle and sat down to talk. I was told that they together had started a program called the Renaissance Project. They had the New Rochelle office and an office in Yonkers, New York. "How many kids do you have?" I asked. "We have twenty but remember we're just getting started. That's where you come in, Al. We'd like you to start as a field representative and go into the streets to recruit members for us." "How many staff do you have?" I asked. "Counting you, Al, we have one, you." We all laughed and then I said, "Joking aside, let's talk money." Freddy looked at Tom and said, "Why does Al always bring up problems?" "Al, we have no money. We're not funded, and all our money comes from donations. We are taking a stipend of 25 dollars a week, our gas and cleaning is paid for by the program. Yours will be the same, but Al, we will get funded soon. I'm working on that now and you'll be coming in on the ground floor of something that's going to be very big."

Later, I was alone thinking. I knew finding a job would be hard, with my police record and the fact that I have not worked since I was a kid of thirteen. Also, this is the work I'd like to do, to help others as I was helped. This work I knew, this I was good at and this is where I belonged. I also was very secure working for friends. I took the job. Money was no issue, we were dedicated. Very dedicated. We worked eighteen hours a day, seven days a week. Soon we were building our population. Kids from all over Westchester County were coming through our doors. We were taking on more staff, all from Daytop. A few months later, we were given an old hotel in Ellenville, New York, to be used as a residential facility. A very rich man whose name I forget bought it and sold it to us for one dollar. The Ellenville facility was a beautiful place. On a guess because it's been so many years, I'd say it had to be located on about ten acres of land. There was a main building, very large, and about ten cottages with a large pool. We now had about one hundred and twenty-five kids. The Yonkers office never did anything and was closed. New Rochelle and Ellenville were thriving. I was now an Assistant Director.

Aside from working with the kids, we set up a parents' organization. I was always out doing speaking engagements and talking to people in the community. I remember once being in my mother's house, putting on a suit and getting ready to do a speaking engagement for about seven, eight or nine hundred people from a parent-teacher association, or PTA for short, and I asked my mother if she would like to come with me. "Yes, indeed," she said. She had become very proud of her son and what a good feeling that was for both of us. As we were driving up to the Bronx for this PTA meeting, I asked her if she would like to speak to the parents. "Mom," I said, "who knows better than you what parents go through with children that use drugs? You'd be great." "Oh, no, you're not getting me up there in front of all those people," my mother said. It was funny, I could convince a kid not to use drugs but I couldn't convince my mother to talk in front of an audience.

We arrived at the school and soon I was called to the podium to speak. My proud mother was in the first row. I gave about a thirty-minute opening, talking about myself and the history of the program. After my opening statement, I would then turn it over for questions and answers but this time I said, "Ladies and gentlemen, I have a problem. Well, not me, my mother has the problem. I know she would love to get up here and speak to all of you explaining what she went through with two sons that used drugs but she's afraid, but I'm sure if you give her a big hand, she will get up."

I now had these seven, eight or nine hundred people clapping for my mother and she walked on stage, got behind the podium and started to speak. I was amazed myself at what came out of her mouth. She talked about how it felt to have two sons, both addicts. She talked about going to work and wondering if she would ever see her sons alive again. She talked about how it felt to have two sons in and out of prison all the time. She spoke about how it felt to visit her sons in prison and talk through a telephone, looking through a glass. She talked about how ashamed she was to see the neighbors and would always walk into the building through the back door when we lived in an apartment building. We lived on Martense St. and she would walk through a building on Linden Blvd, across the courtyard and into our building through the back door so she wouldn't have to see anyone. She talked about feeling like the stairs were shaking under her when she walked up to the third floor and always wondering if she would find her sons alive or dead. She talked about crying at night, almost every night.

I sat behind her feeling so guilty. I had never heard this but I was able to understand it. I realized then how selfish I had been, how I was only thinking of myself and nobody around me counted. How I destroyed not only me but also the people around me that loved me. Aunts, uncles and cousins. My family was not thought of through those years; my only thought was how to get my hands on more drugs. It's a shame but it's the truth, we hurt the ones we love. She thanked everyone for listening and walked off the stage. I took the podium but didn't say a word till she got to her seat. Finally, she sat down and I was stuck for words. I said, "Before I go on, let me say to my mother that I am sorry, very sorry. I never realized any of this and we will talk about this on the way home." We did speak about it in the car going home. "It's over, Allan," she said. "There's no need to feel guilty, you had problems, now just make me proud." We rushed home to catch a T.V. program I had taped a few days before and got home just in time. We both enjoyed watching me talk about the relationship between parents and children that are involved with drugs. I started to think that maybe she should have been the one to tape the T.V. show.

Soon Renaissance became funded and payments were made retroactively going back six months. I was living with the parents of a kid that was in our residential facility, my dear friends Ralph and Millie of Port Chester and now Rye, New York. They became family to me and I was spending time between their house and my mother's in Brooklyn.

One day Freddy was talking to the powers-to-be of Daytop and he started to tell them I was with him and doing good. I just happened to be walking into Freddy's office at the time and he handed me the phone. I motioned to him, "Who's this?" "Billy, from Daytop," he said. "Hey, Billy, how are ya?" We spoke for a while and Billy tried to get me to come back to Daytop. "I don't think you are ready, Al," Billy stated. "Billy, I'm ready and in time I will prove that to you and if I ever walk in your office again, it will be as an equal not as a resident. I'm handing the phone back to Fred but Billy I'd like to be able to stay in contact with you." "Sure, Al, good luck," said Billy.

One day I was called to Freddy's office. Freddy said to me, "Al, I'm having problems in Ellenville and I'm pulling the director out. I'd like to send you up there as the director." "Sure," I said, "no problem." Although I always wanted to run the Ellenville facility, I never did say anything but

I always liked working with the hardcore addicts rather than the kid who smoked pot or took a few pills.

My social life wasn't going so well. I dated some, but still hadn't found that one special lady, the one you think about during work, the one you rush home to every night because you just want to be with her. So going back to the Catskills wasn't a problem. I loved working in Ellenville; I loved everything about it, except that now I was in the same situation I had been in at Swan Lake. I was lonely. Here, I wasn't dating at all.

Soon we opened another facility in Westport, Connecticut. That facility had its own Board of Directors. The Board of Directors in New York had nothing to do with the Westport facility. My friend Rick was running that facility and doing a good job, only he couldn't communicate with the Board of Directors and never answered their phone calls and they wanted him out. You guessed it. I soon found myself in Westport, Connecticut. I liked Westport. What a nice town in a beautiful county, Fairfield County. I built it up from just a few kids to about fifty in a short time, always keeping in mind that we can't grow too fast for fear of having too much of a negative influence within the facility. As in New Rochelle, we started a parents' organization.

Things were going very well in Westport, including my social life. I was dating a lot and, for the first time, I felt like I had a life. This is what I had left Daytop for, to have a place to live, a job and a social life. This was my objective, my goal, and finally it was here and what a great feeling it was. Now I was like everyone else living in society. I felt whole. I soon met a lady that I had liked very much and started to date her exclusively. It was she and I. She lived about twenty minutes from Westport in Greenwich, Connecticut, and we developed a great relationship. We saw each other almost every evening and things, I thought, were going great. After a few months, we got engaged and my family, being so happy for me, threw us an engagement party. My mother was on top of the world. Not only did her son change his life, making her very proud, but now she could look ahead and hope for a grandchild or two and maybe three. "I'm not a machine, mom." Things were going great for me. I had a good woman that I loved, a job that I loved, working in a town that I loved and I thought everything was fine.

A few months went by and we were talking about setting a date and I couldn't have been happier. She was the woman that had me thinking of her during the day, the woman that had me running to see her after work, the woman I wanted to spend my life loving. One day I called her office and the receptionist answered the phone as always. I had spoken to this person so many times but had never met her. I asked for my girlfriend and she said, "Al, Karen called us today. She won't be back till Monday." I said, "What are you talking about, she won't be back till Monday?" "Al," she said, "I hate to be the one to tell you this but Karen ran off and married her ex-boyfriend. She called about an hour ago and told us that she will be back Monday." I was crushed. My first thoughts were thank God I didn't marry this girl and that's just what I told the woman on the phone. I thanked her for telling me and hung up. I sat back in my chair with tears coming out of my eyes. I never saw this coming, I had no idea. I never thought this could happen. We were, I thought, so happy together. In the next few days I started to put all the gifts from the engagement party together and returned them all, thanking people for their good wishes.

Work went on as always. I was hurt but I had responsibilities and a facility to run, and that came first. About a month later, I was giving a seminar to the parents' organization and someone came over and whispered to me. "Someone in the hall is here to see you." "Ask them to come in," I said. "No, they won't come in," I was told. "Tell them I'll be finished in a few minutes and I'll come out into the hall." "Who was this mystery guest?" I wondered. I finished my seminar and walked into the hall and it was Karen, my ex-girlfriend. "What brings you here?" I asked. "Things didn't work out for me," she said. "Did you expect they would?" I said. "The whole thing was wrong, what you did was wrong and the way you did it was wrong. Didn't you ever learn that things must be done the right way if they are going to work out? Didn't you ever learn that dirt turns to dirt and that love is a clean thing? You can't mix the two together." "Is there a chance we can get back together?" she said. "Are you seeing anyone?" "No, I'm not seeing anyone but still there is no chance of us ever getting back together. I'm sorry Karen but I could never trust you again. I have to get back to my meeting, I wish you the best," and I walked away.

I still loved Karen and couldn't stop thinking about her and this was very hard for me to do, only I loved me more than I loved her and I wasn't selling out. That had to be one of the hardest things I ever did but I had to do it. It didn't make me feel any better but it did make me feel stronger. I had always thought I would melt if I saw her again but

I didn't melt and I stuck to my convictions. She wasn't right for me and I knew it. Her own mother told me after we broke up, "Allan, you have no idea how lucky you are." Obviously, there was more to Karen than I knew and that upset me. I was the guy who knew people, that could read people. Did love blind me? Did I want something so bad that I couldn't see reality? Could this happen again? A scary thought but one that I had to look at and think about.

A while later, Freddy left Renaissance and started working for a program set up by the City of New York. The program was called Addiction Services Agency, or A.S.A. for short. One evening, I received a call from Freddy who told me he had something good for me. I drove down to his house and we talked. Freddy had a powerful position with A.S.A. "I got something I think you'll be interested in, programming and evaluation for seventeen facilities." "A lot of responsibility," I thought. I also wouldn't be working with the kids. I'd be directing the staff, evaluating them, teaching them and pumping new life into their facilities, always evaluating everything around me. The money was more than I was making at the time but that wasn't the selling point. The important thing was, where can I do the most good? In Renaissance, I directed one facility and taught about 50 kids. In ASA, I could teach hundreds by working with the staff. With that, I took the job with the City of New York where I was able to reach kids in seventeen facilities. I would visit each facility and work with the staff but always found time to talk to the kids. That was my passion, the kids. Helping them, guiding them, teaching them and, of course, joking with them. I also spent a lot of time behind my desk sending memos around and communicating by phone. This I didn't like. I wanted to be on the front line, but I did my job and handled my responsibility.

I started dating again and met this woman that lived in New York City while I was now living back in Brooklyn and we dated a few times. She kept telling me about her roommate. "Oh, you have to meet my roommate; she's such a nice person." Well, one day while picking her up at her apartment, I walked in and there was my ex-girlfriend Karen sitting there. "Are you Sophie's roommate?" I asked. "Yeah," she told me. "It's a small world we live in," was my reply. We spoke for a while. It was nice, it was friendly and there was nothing said about our relationship whatsoever and I was glad about that. Soon I stopped seeing Sophie, the girl I was dating.

It was really nothing more then a sexual relationship and I felt it was better not to see Karen again because I still had some feelings for her.

Soon Fred was calling me into the office again and he told me, "I have this facility in Brooklyn on 4th Ave. that I want you to take charge of for a while till I get someone to run it. We're having some problems there and I want to move the two people out that are running it now. Build it up again and then, once that's done, you'll come back to your job and I'll put someone else in there." The next day I went down to the facility and spoke to the outgoing staff. They were visibly upset but not at me, at Fred. They left huffing and puffing and I took a look around. I called a house meeting and introduced myself. Then I spent the next couple of days talking to kids one-on-one. I saw no sign of any problems other than one. Not one kid expressed any displeasure about those two guys leaving and that seemed odd to me. A director of a program becomes a father figure to his kids. Why didn't these kids care that the father figure was gone? Why were they so eager to accept me? This was one mystery I wanted to solve and one that I did solve.

I found no mistreatment, no abuse and nothing out of the ordinary so one day I confronted Fred. I asked why he got rid of those two guys. "Freddy," I said, "the facility is running well, the kids are happy, learning and doing just what they're supposed to. Each kid is at the point that he or she is supposed to be for the length of time they're around." "Drop it, Al. It's not your business." "Wait a minute, Fred. You mean to tell me that as long as we know each other and as close as we worked together for so many years, I can't confront you about certain things, especially when it's about the facility I'm running and the kids I'm working with?" A few more words were exchanged and I went back to the facility to investigate further and I found that the kids weren't too upset because they had known for a while that these two guys were leaving. Obviously, there was a conflict between Fred and these two guys. Well, you don't fire people because you're having a conflict with them. The main reason we're here is for the kids and if these guys, conflict or not, are doing their job well and the kids are getting what they're supposed to, you find a way to smooth out any differences. Sometimes you can and sometimes you can't, but you don't take it out on the kids. These guys did a good job and there was no reason to relieve them of their duties.

I went back to the facility and continued on with my job. While I was working, in Connecticut there were certain things taking place that would someday affect me. The Mayor of Norwalk called in the director of the Board of Health and the Police Chief for a meeting. The Mayor wanted them to set up a committee and start looking for the right drug rehabilitation program to bring into his town. They formed a committee and started to investigate various programs. Soon the consensus was to bring in a program run by an ex-addict. They felt, as I do, that programs run by ex-addicts are the most effective programs going and for three obvious reasons:

One: who knows more than an ex-addict what an addict needs to change his life? He's been there, he's lived it.

Two: these kids can't lie to us. Any lie they tell us we told ten or fifteen years before they even thought about telling that lie.

Three: who can be more passionate and more dedicated to helping these kids than someone who's been there and knows what these kids are going through and what lies ahead of them?

I'd like to know which professional would work eighteen hours a day, seven days a week, for twenty-five dollars a week and gas money. No, there can never be anyone with the dedication and wisdom of the ex-addict. Once the committee decided that a therapeutic community run by an ex-addict was the proper program for Norwalk, they started to look around for the person to run this program. I don't know how many people they interviewed. I don't even know if they interviewed anyone. I do know that they approached Renaissance (Westport) and asked them to expand into Norwalk. Renaissance refused, stating they weren't in a position to expand at that time but they did recommend me.

I received a call from an attorney who explained that he was a member of the committee. His name was Frank and we were on a first name basis right away. He went on to say that Norwalk, with the help of the Mayor, wanted to put a program in their town. He explained that this committee would one day become the Board of Directors for this program. He asked me if I would be willing to move back to that area and start a program of my own. Frank also told me that there would be no interference from the Board of Directors. It would be my program, unless of course there were problems. That was understandable as there has to be a governing body. We talked for about another ten minutes. "I can set up an appointment for you to meet with the committee if you choose in favor of this," he said. I said, "I would be willing to drive up and meet with the Board and exchange ideas." At this point they wanted to learn about me and I wanted to learn about them. They wanted to know how I would run this program and they wanted to know my background concerning drugs. Along with that, they also wanted to know what experience I had in this field of recovery.

I had questions also. I wanted to know what they meant by, it's my program to run my way. I needed no interference from people who knew nothing about this problem or how to solve a problem a kid may have. I also wanted to know where the money to run this program was coming from and I also wanted to talk about salary. The conversation ended with Frank telling me he would set up a meeting and get back to me.

A few days later Frank called back, and now I knew that they were serious. Frank and I exchanged pleasantries and spoke for a while. He said he wanted me to come to his office and meet with a few members of the Board for a preliminary meeting. I drove up and met the people involved. They all seemed very nice. I didn't get into too much that day. If I got through this committee, I would save my questions for the entire Board. They asked about me and my history of drug abuse and I told them. They then asked about my experience working with others. I told them and also handed them a copy of my resume. We spoke for a while, they left and then Frank and I talked for about fifteen minutes. "They liked you, Al. I can tell," Frank said. "Well, Frank, they have good taste," I said, and we both laughed.

I headed back to Brooklyn where I lived on E.8 St between Ave. H and I. Frank and I were getting friendly by now. He called once just to tell me that they were setting up a meeting for the entire Board to meet me. Frank was a young, sharp attorney that knew his way around a courtroom. He then called a third time and gave me the address of the Health Department in Norwalk and told me when to be there. When I arrived, they were all seated around a conference table, the president of the Board at the head of the table, and I on his right. I was introduced to everyone around the table and we spoke. Once again, I was answering the same questions I had answered before but this time they wanted to know in detail how the program would be run. I explained step-by-step the functioning of the program. I explained how kids come in and start at the bottom of the ladder. I explained how they move up from one department to another. I went on to talk about the different departments we have in the facility: The Service Crew, the Kitchen Crew, Maintenance Crew, the Business office, Expediting Team, Procurement Team, and the Coordinating Team. I explained the functions of each department and why each department has a department head and a ramrod (foreman). I spoke about the group encounter sessions and marathon sessions. I talked about rewarding for good behavior and disciplining for bad behavior. I explained about the status of being a ramrod, a department head, an expediter, a coordinator and a group leader. I explained how status is even in the bedrooms. When a kid comes in, he's given the lower bunk. As he shows that he's trying, that he's following the path to getting himself together, he's moved to the top bunk, then, finally, to the single bed. Once in the single, he's considered the strength of the room and it's his responsibility to see to it that the room is clean. Each member of the room does his or her part to get that room cleaned. They all have their jobs and all chip in to clean the room.

Then I asked some questions of my own. What is meant by I run this program? Where is the money coming from to support this program and if I take this position what would my salary be? They told me that it is my program to be run the way I see fit and that there would be no interference from them. They told me that the City of Norwalk is giving them five thousand dollars seed money but it will be their responsibility to raise the money. They also had a storefront facility that was being renovated. It had been an old radio station that burned in a fire. My job was just to run the program; all other responsibilities were theirs. Then they said my starting salary would be 13,000 dollars a year. "Thirteen thousand a year," I said. "The number 13 scares me. Can you make that 13,001 dollars?" Someone handed me a dollar and I said, "You have a deal." The money wasn't great and, at the same time, it wasn't bad. It did afford me the opportunity to direct my own program, to put some of my own ideas to work, to create a program that's a life-giving tool for all drug abusers no matter where they came from, no matter what color they were, no matter what religion they were and for those that don't practice religion. Young and old, big and small, anybody and everybody that wants help will be able to get it. After the meeting Frank offered me a drink and the Chief of Police joined us. Can you imagine? Here I was, having a drink with the chief of police. Boy, how things have changed.

The year was 1970 and, on the trip home, I started to think of my accomplishments over the past four years and I was rather pleased. In four years, I had gone from a convicted drug user in a penitentiary to the director of a drug rehabilitation program. I named the program Operation S.P.E.A.R., which stood for Special Prevention Education and Recovery. I returned to New York, handed in my resignation and started making arrangements to move. I called a friend of mine who was in real estate in the Westport, Connecticut area and he got me an apartment right off Interstate 95 in Westport, Connecticut, just north of Norwalk.

Soon I was moving up to Connecticut. I moved into my apartment, and at 9 A.M. sharp on Monday morning, I was at my new office at the Health Department in Norwalk. I was using the Health Department until my storefront was finished with its renovations. I walked in, set things up in my office, unpacked my belongings that were going into my office and sat down at the desk. I sat there, and I sat there, and I sat there, not knowing where to start. Where to start? What to do? Where to go? I'm here, now what? I realized then that I hadn't put much thinking into how to start and I better get right into it.

I knew I couldn't really get started until I had a facility. There was no way I could bring a bunch of drug users into the Health Department, so I started contacting old friends that I knew when I worked for the Renaissance Project in Westport. I met with the head of the Probation Department in Norwalk and in Bridgeport. I had contacted a couple of judges that had helped me keep kids in the program I had run before. The idea is that once a kid gets arrested, I would go to court and represent this kid, not as his attorney, but as a director of a drug rehabilitation program. The defendant would be placed on probation with a stipulation that he or she enter and remain in the program. Leaving prematurely would consti-tute a violation of that probation. That way, we would have some time to work with this kid. I started to call attorneys in town. I spoke to everyone I could think of that would come in contact with drug abusers.

Now I was playing the waiting game, waiting for my storefront to be finished. Once I got word that it was ready, I moved in as fast as I could. I stood outside the office one day and noticed the Norwalk newspaper was across the street so I walked over there. "Hi. My name is Allan Rykoff and I just started a new drug rehabilitation program right across the street and would like to tell the people of Norwalk that we're here and eager to help their sons or daughters, neighbors and friends who have a drug abuse problem." One reporter that was there was at the meeting the evening I got hired and had done a story on my hiring, only I was back in New York and unaware of this. "Sure, Al, no problem. Let me put something together for you. I'll walk it across the street when it's finished for your approval and anything we can do to help, just call on us," the reporter said.

The next day, a really beautiful article was in the paper telling the people of Norwalk that we're here to serve them. I had also contacted everyone I spoke to in the past to let them know our doors were open and I sat back and waited. Nothing happened and I was getting nervous. I have this facility, I have the ability to help people, but I have no people to help. Four weeks went by and nothing. I was starting to worry, starting to think, "Did I do the right thing? Can I make this thing work?" My inadequacies started to pop up. Am I smart enough, do I have the education for this? Where am I going wrong? What am I doing wrong? What part of the puzzle am I missing? Over and over, I questioned myself and I was wracking my brain. All those people that promised their help, where are they? The attorneys, the probation departments, the judges, where are they now that I'm open? I put a program here in the middle of town and all I have is an empty storefront.

I was sitting in front of my house near Interstate 95 and saw a sign. It read "New York" with an arrow pointing to the highway. "Was this a sign for me?" I asked myself. Every inadequacy I had started to pop up. Was I really stupid, what am I missing, why can't I get kids in my program? What's wrong with me? I thought about it and thought about it. Give up now, that's crazy. I can make this work but it's going to take time. I can't just give up, I have to stay here and fight this temptation to go back. Just then I heard the phone ring. I walked into the house and it was my mother. The one person I didn't want to hear from right now. "Everything is fine, mom, going good. It takes time. I'll get there. You just don't worry; everything is fine," I explained to my mother.

At the next board meeting, I asked for another staff member. "Another staff member?" they asked. "How many kids do you have now?" "One, and that's the reason I need another staff member. I have to run around, I have to hang out in the courthouses. I have to meet with probation and parole. I have to speak to judges. I have to do speaking engagements and so much more and I need someone in the office to be there when I'm not." Finally, my request was granted.

After months of communicating with Daytop, I was now allowed back on their property, so I went back and hired my friend Bobby who was a staff member for them. Now I was free to run around and I was doing a lot of talking. From Greenwich to Bridgeport, I was meeting everyone I could. I was talking to anyone that would talk to me. Slowly kids came trickling in. Five, ten, fifteen and soon we had about fifty. Bobby was offered a very good job in New York and took it so I hired someone else. The Probation Department, along with the courts, was starting to send me kids but what they were sending were hardcore addicts and a daycare facility is not geared for the hardcore. You can't teach a kid who's using hard drugs during the day and send him home in the evening time. In most cases, that kid will be high before he gets to his door and everything you said to him will have gone out the window. As these hardcore addicts were walking through the door, I was sending them to other programs that had residential facilities. I now had about thirty pot abusers that I was able to work with effectively in a daycare setting but the hardcore were all being sent to other facilities.

Operation S.P.E.A.R. still had no funding and we were living off donations that I would get when doing speaking engagements or talking to civic organizations. At the next Board of Directors meeting, I announced that we had a need for a residential facility. I told the Board how I was funneling kids from our program to other programs and if we were going to call ourselves a full service program, we then would have to open a residential facility. They thought I was crazy. "Al, we don't have money to run this facility. How can we take on a new responsibility? Where would the money come from?" "I'll tell you how. What if I come up with a facility, rent-free, and what if I show you letters from every member of our parents organization offering food, clothing, furniture and whatever else is needed to run this house, would you, the Board of Directors, give me permission to open that facility and would you, the Board, come up with the money for the electric and telephone? That's all I need from you, the electric and the telephone. I will do the rest." My Board, thinking I was a dreamer, said, "Yes."

I contacted a realtor friend of mine asking for his help. I explained what I needed, a large house with at least thirty to forty rooms with some acreage. The next day I got a call from him telling me he'd located a large facility on four acres of land about 50 miles away. We drove up and looked at the house. It was so beautiful, one of the most beautiful houses I have ever seen in my entire life. "What are you asking?" I asked. "Two and a half million," was the answer the woman gave me. I said, "Thank you very much for your time, but it's just out of our price range," and we left. On the way home, I spoke to the realtor again about what we needed and how I hoped to work this out. He now had a better understanding about our needs.

A week or two later, the realtor called again. He was all excited. "Al, I think I got the answer. I'll pick you up at the office." He picked me up and we drove only eight miles to the next town of Wilton. Here, on the main road, Route 7 if I remember correctly, was a 27-room house with a 4-room cottage in the back that had been used as a convalescent home. We walked around. It had bedrooms on the second and third floors. One very large room also was on the second floor, which I figured would be the director's office. The kitchen was large enough to accommodate fifty to sixty people. The two buildings sat on 6 acres of land. "What's the price?" I asked. "It's not for sale; it's a rental," the realtor told me. "Five hundred a month." I turned to the realtor and said, "It's got a basketball hoop, huh? What a selling point, I'm a fan. I want this house." "Can you put the numbers together?" he asked. He knew our situation because I had just explained to him in detail about it and he really wanted to help because I was going out with his cousin and we became good friends. "Tell the owner I'll work it out but he has to give me a week or two to call an emergency Board meeting. This facility is mine," I said. "You work with the owner; I'll put the rest together," I added.

I wanted this facility; it was just what we needed. It had the number of rooms we needed, the space we needed. A large kitchen and living room and the acreage we needed. The only thing that could have made it better was more bedrooms, but the rooms were large and I knew we could put a single bed along with a bunk bed in each room, giving us three to a room. I was excited. I felt like a baby with a new toy. Now I knew that if I got this facility, I could do the work I needed to do to help all the people that needed us. I also knew it would be that much easier to get funded when the time for that came. All the pieces were falling into place.

Now all I had to do was get someone to pay the rent until we got funded and this had to be done fast. I wanted the doors opened as soon as possible. Where was that someone? Who was that someone? I knew if I went to food distributors I could get food, with clothing manufacturers I could get clothing but the rent, that was the thing that boggled my mind. An extra $500 a month when you're living on donations was not easy to come up with. I thought about going to the city of Norwalk and telling them, "Hey, you wanted a drug rehabilitation program, you got one. Now dig in your pockets and pay for it," but there was a problem there. The residential facility wasn't in the city of Norwalk; it was in the city of Wilton. Would that present a problem? I wasn't sure. "Could I bring the two Mayors together for a meeting? This could work," I thought. Neither of them would want to be the first to say "No" and I'd probably wind up with a "Yes." I was very friendly with the Mayor of Norwalk, my good friend Frank, whose idea it was to start this program in the first place. "Was this ethical?" I thought. "What I'd be doing is manipulating the system." Was it right to put either of these guys in that position? It could work or it could turn into a political nightmare. I had to think about this one real hard. Is there any other way? Let me leave the two cities on the burner and think of another way. My brain seemed overwhelmed, my head was spinning. God, please find me a way, just give me an idea; I'll do the rest. Then it dawned on me, a civic organization.

Before the Board meeting, I called a member of my Board who was also a member of the Kiwanis Club. I explained what I had found and told him that I'd like to address the Kiwanis Club. "Sure, Al, I'll get back to you with a date," he said. I met with and addressed the Kiwanis Club and presented my case. This is what we have now, this is what we need and this, with your help, is what we can have. I explained the need for this facility and how it would benefit the entire community. I spoke and I spoke watching people's faces to get an idea of how they were receiving me. It was hard to tell. The meeting ended, I thanked them for listening and left.

A few days after speaking to them, my Board member called me saying the Kiwanis Club would donate 5,000 dollars by paying the rent for ten months. "I did it," I thought to myself. "That's all I need." I said, "I can put this together." Later that week, at a parents' organization meeting, I asked for letters of promises for clothing, furniture, food and more. The last step, my Board of Directors. They made a commitment thinking I was a dreamer. Now they're going to find out that dreams do come true. Will they back out or will they keep their word? A Board meeting was held and I presented my case. "Last month I spoke to you about the need for a residential facility, I'm sure you remember that. Well, I have come up with a facility that can house 50 to 60 kids on six acres of land not too far from here, in Wilton. The Kiwanis Club has offered their help with a 5,000 dollar donation that will pay the rent for ten months. I have in this folder letters of promise from each parent and some storekeepers in town to donate food, clothing, furniture, toiletries and other items. Ladies and gentlemen, I am ready to open the operation S.P.E.A.R. residential facility." I never had to say "check last month's minutes where it says you would agree to this if I found a building." They knew it and had no choice but to agree to it now. Truth is, they never expected I would come up with this building but I knew I wasn't giving up till I did. This is what the hard-core needed and I was in business to help all that needed help.

I left that meeting feeling so good, so proud and now I had to call the number one person in my life. "Hi, mom, how are you?" My mom said, "What's the matter? Why are you calling so late, Allan?" "I have some good news. I now have a residential facility." She was as excited as I was. "When can I see it?" she asked. "I don't know. Can you paint?" "No." "Can you move furniture?" "No." "Can you drive a truck?" "No." "Well, then, I guess you'll have to wait till all that is done," I explained to my mother. She knows me long enough to know I was playing with her and she was so happy, so proud, and that made me feel so great.

Once I got the keys, I organized a paint party. We put on the stereo and ordered some pizzas. A paint party without pizza, never happen. I had parents, members of the program and friends of the program help paint this large facility and they did a great job. Inside and out, the two buildings shined. Everyone was enjoying himself, everyone knew that the work they were doing now would help save lives soon. Now donations of food, clothing, furniture, dishes, silverware, clothing, food, toiletries, televisions, radios and so much more were pouring in. They were coming in by the truckload. The Norwalk community opened their hearts, cleaned out their houses and donated it all. Beds, blankets, pillows, sheets, towels and food kept coming for a few weeks and we were stocked up. It took about two weeks before we were ready to open our doors and I hung a sign right on the main road in front of the house. "The family of S.P.E.A.R."

The courts, judges, attorneys and the Probation Department knew we had opened; I had lots of friends there. We started to grow slowly, ten, twenty, thirty, and then we cut it off. We didn't want too much of a negative influence in the facility. We needed these kids to grow some before we brought others in. These kids, the ones we had now, would soon become the strength for the others. These were the kids who would run the data to the new people coming in. They would guide the new kids, teach them what they learned but, first, they needed to learn themselves. At that point, my title had changed from Director to Executive Director. To be honest, I liked that title and it was needed because I now had two other directors, one at the daycare center and one at the residential facilities.

Still not funded, it was a battle to keep this program afloat. I was running all over town trying to raise money. I must have spoken to every civic group around, every organization and so many businesses. I never stopped. I talked to whoever would listen, and I guess even some that didn't want to listen, always trying to raise money to keep this going and the community was great. No kid ever missed a meal or had to wear shabby clothing. What really helped was the fact that the rent was paid. That Kiwanis Club donation was the key to the entire thing.

A few weeks later, I approached an all-black funding agency in Norwalk for money. Norwalk, at that time, had a problem between whites and blacks but that didn't bother me. I needed money to help all the people, not just whites. They did have one white guy on staff and I spoke to him in his office. "What chance do I have to get some money from this agency?" I asked him. "You don't have a shot in hell," he said. Stu was right. I was turned down.

A few weeks after that, while I was sitting at my desk, my secretary (a resident at the residential facility) called and said, "A fellow by the name of Stu is here to see you." "Send him in," I said. It was this same guy Stu who worked for that funding agency. After saying our hellos, I asked, "Stu, what can I do for you?" and his reply was, "I want to do for you. I want to help you put a proposal together to be presented to the federal government." "You got time for this, Stu? It's going to take months to put this together!" "Al," he said, "I just got fired and I have all the time in the world." I told him, "Fine, and when we write this proposal, we will put you in as my administrative assistant. If we get funded, you have a job. If we don't, I can't promise you anything." Stu agreed. My next step was to contact the Executive Director of Daytop. There was now a new Executive Director at Daytop and I knew him well. He was my probation officer when I entered Daytop the first time. I called him and told him that Stu and I would like to meet with him. "Tomorrow, O.K.?" he asked. "Tomorrow is fine. I look forward to seeing you," I said. He and I were in contact throughout the years. He was very friendly with the Renaissance project that I had worked for and we were good friends.

Funding and writing proposals was so far over my head it wasn't funny. I had been out of school since I was thirteen and never paid attention while I was there, and the ADD wasn't helping me. Stu was a God sent. During this meeting, we found out who to contact in Washington, how to get the application and what type of funding was best for us. Stu and I locked in his house for about four months and I explained in detail every aspect of this program and Stu just read my mind. He had a knack for putting things on paper. I would explain why we had a Service Crew, why we had a Maintenance Crew, why we had a Business Office, a Kitchen Crew, a Procurement Team, Expediters and Coordinators, why we have group encounter, why we have morning meeting, why we have seminars, why we have marathon sessions, why we have discussion groups, why we have Open House and so much more, just like I had told my Board of Directors in my interview. Only with Stu, I went even deeper into each aspect of the program. He had to really grasp it, to be able to put it down on paper in a way that those that will be reading it can understand it. Then Stu would write. While he was writing, I was running to check on my daycare and residential facilities. In the evening time, I was doing speaking engagements and fund-raising. I now had about five staff members and things there were going good. We had about fifty kids at the daycare facility and were growing at the residential facility. I knew we could house about 55 residents at the residential facility, and that basically is what we had once we grew to that point.

It took Stu and me the better part of four months to put this proposal together. Now we had to get it typed. I had a friend Connie who was the secretary to the Vice President of Xerox in Stamford, Connecticut. I gave her the papers, 160 pages in all. "Do your magic," I said. Well, my dear friend Connie types so good it sounds like a piano playing. She called me when it was finished and said, "Al, all we have to do now is copy it, bind it and label it, and then you're good to go. How many copies do you need?" I told her that I needed 20, plus the original for the funding agency, 20 for the Board of Directors and an extra 20 to hold." She said, "Get your binders and labels and pick me up at my house at 7:00 P.M. this evening." Connie had gotten permission for us to do this in the evening time. Stu, two kids from the house and I went to pick up Connie at her home and drove down to Stamford. She took us to the copy room where they had this very impressive-looking machine. It was almost the length of the room. She put the papers in and it copied and collated. Now all we had to do was bind them and label them. "What a great machine," I told Connie. "This is Xerox," she said.

The following day, Stu, who now had an office next to mine, came in and sat down. "Al, these papers have to be in Maryland tomorrow or we have to wait till next year. I'll book us a flight." "A flight?" I asked. "Can't we go by boat? Stu, I've never flown. The only plane I've seen close up was one that crashed on Rikers Island. Now you're telling me I have to fly." "Don't worry, you'll love it." he said. Sarcastically I said, "Sure I will Stu. Get the hell out of my office, book the fight and leave me alone while I pray." Stu laughed and walked out. The following day, I found myself at Kennedy Airport. We boarded the plane and I said, "Stu, let me sit by the window, I want to keep my eye on the propeller and God help us if it stops turning." I was looking out the window and it was really so beautiful but I still wasn't relaxed. I heard a noise. "What's that, Stu?" "Don't worry the wheels just went up." We landed in DCA, Washington's Airport, and took a cab to the headquarters of the National Institute of Mental Health in Maryland, which today is N.I.D.A., the National Institute of Drug Abuse. We spoke to someone for about an hour and handed in 21 copies of our application for funding. One original and 20 copies. We flew back that same day. The plane took off and we heard a noise. Stu said, "What's that, Al?" "Don't worry Stu, the wheels just went up." "You're an old hand at this," he said. "Stu, as soon as we land, I'm joining the Air Force."

After we returned, Stu kept writing. He now knew just about everything there was to know about the functioning of a program and, while he wrote, I was running back and forth between the daycare facility where our offices were and the residential facility. I was meeting with judges, with probation, parole and anyone or any other department that I thought might have kids that needed help in an effort to keep the lines of communication open. There were a few programs doing the same, and I wanted to be the first program these people think about when they have a kid in front of them that needs a program, and we did became the number one program around. We had so many friends in so many organizations.

We went to Hartford and submitted a proposal to the state of Connecticut. We submitted another one to the city of Norwalk. Along with this, I was doing about three speaking engagements a week, talking to PTA's, civic groups, women's clubs, churches, synagogues and so many more. Every group was helping us financially and it caused a little problem. Although it kept us going financially, because that's all we had at the time, it caused problems another way. These groups always wanted their picture in the paper handing me a check. At one Board meeting, I was confronted. "Al, you have to stay out of the papers. We're a non-profit organization and people will think we're rich." "It's not me," I said. "These organizations want the publicity. We need the money, how can I say no?"

Giving money to operation S.P.E.A.R. became the new trend in town but the reality was that we still didn't have enough. Keep in mind, we housed over 50 kids and had another 50 at the daycare facility. If you ever raised children, then you know the cost, times a 100. They didn't give much, five hundred, a thousand, some times twenty five hundred, if we were lucky, but ever dime went for the program. Aside from the parents' group, we started a siblings group for brothers and sisters of our members. That wasn't too successful but we did what we could.

The local radio station in town asked me to do a show every Sunday morning at 8:00 A.M, a question and answer show where people would call in, ask questions about drug abuse and I would answer their questions. At a Board meeting about two months later, the Board asked how the radio show was going. "I'm not sure," I said. "I'm getting a lot of callers but I'm hearing the same voices: and a few of the Board members started to laugh. The Chairman of the Board said, "My wife calls 3 to 4 times every show." Someone else said, "My husband called twice last week," and there was more." "O.K.," I said. "It's obvious that people aren't interested in drug abuse on Sunday morning at 8:00 A.M. so I'm going to take the show off the air and sleep a little later on Sunday." They knew I put in my hours. For the first year the Chairman of the Board would call me every day at a different time. Sometimes in the morning, sometimes during the day and sometimes late at night, and I was always there or at a speaking engagement or a meeting and I always called him back as soon as I returned to the office.

I sat back one day and looked at the entire program. We had grown fast and we were the number one program in the state. I was so proud of my accomplishments. I remembered when I started, the first month when I looked at the sign pointing to New York and how I wondered if I had made the right decision coming to Norwalk. Now I knew I had. My mother and my entire family were proud and I was in contact with all of them. During my years of drug abuse, I very rarely saw my aunts and uncles. I never went to family functions. I was either too busy chasing the drugs or in jail, and family had become secondary. Now it was different, now I was not only back but I was very respected by all of them. They saw what happened to my brother. They were all at his funeral and they were so glad to have me happy, healthy and in good spirits. They witnessed my rise from ashes to become a well-rounded individual. I felt very good about that because I do have a great family, good people who always stayed within the law. My brother and I were the only two that took another route. It was a good feeling being back. I had lost many years but we all knew I had so many years before me that would be shared with them and that pleased us all. I started visiting them, having dinner at their homes and sharing all the good times.

Back at the program, I now had staff that was very capable, which afforded me some time, time to think about me. I decided to go back to school and get my GED. "Here I am," I said, "the head of a program that saves lives." I now had eleven staff members working for me and I should at least have some sort of diploma. I signed up for a course at night in a high school in Norwalk, bought some books and went to school and found myself in the same situation I had been in as a child. No, I wasn't in the last row, last seat, but I could not concentrate. I was now older, smarter and more mature, but soon I realized that I was getting nothing from books. I had known that for a long time but I wanted my GED and figured maybe after all these years, things would have changed. Tell me something or show me something and I don't forget it, but for me to open a book, it's useless; but I didn't drop out. I stayed the course trying to get as much as I could. Although it hurt all over again, I now was old enough and smart enough to understand it, to understand that I had ADD but, as I learned in Daytop, you don't give up. You hang in there and do your best but you don't throw your hands up. After a few months in school, I then signed up for the test. The test was given in Stamford, Connecticut. There were five tests in all, three on one Saturday and the other two on the following Saturday.

The tests were reading comprehension but that didn't throw me either. I was determined. The test went like this: You read a paragraph and you're asked a question about it and circle one of five answers, 1, 2, 3, 4, or 5. I finished all three tests feeling real confident the first Saturday. I drove home after the tests feeling good. "I'm going to pass," I told myself. "I'm going to do this." The following Saturday, I returned for the final two tests. I took the first test and again it was reading comprehension. I felt confident after finishing that also. "Yeah, one more to go," I thought. "I can do it."

The papers for the last test were handed out and it was math. I glanced at the test paper and my heart went out. My God, what is all this? There were things there I never had seen before. They told us to start and I knocked off the two addition and subtraction questions. The two division questions I also finished and was confident that I had gotten those right. The rest of the test was algebra and geometry. I looked at the paper and said to myself, "I have no idea what they're even asking me here. I had not even taken this in school and now, after all these tests that I felt so good about, here I stand with this math test and a good chance of failing. What do I do?" I thought. "I'm not failing," I said. "I've got to figure this out." Well, there was no way to figure it out. You don't just walk into a classroom and figure out algebra and geometry when you have never even seen it before so I decided to guess. "If I skip around circling number 1 here and number 3 there, I'm bound to fail," I thought, so I decided to check number 3 all the way down on both pages. I was the first one that finished, and sat back in my chair. "Are you finished?" the tester asked. "Yes, Ma'am." "Then hand in your paper and you can leave," the tester said. I handed her my paper and left.

A sad feeling came over me as I drove back to Norwalk, "I had failed again," I thought. School wasn't my thing. It brought back so many sad memories of years past, the years in elementary school and junior high school when I would fail my tests or when I was so confused about them that I just stopped and took a failing mark. "I wasn't the bad kid any more but I still failed," I thought. It's sad, I was sad. I kept thinking of how bad I wanted to pass, how bad I wanted that GED but now it didn't look like I'd have it.

Later that night, my girlfriend and I were out for dinner. "You failed, didn't you?" she asked. "How do you know?" "It's written on your face," she said. "Yeah, I failed. I wanted to accomplish this so bad. I wanted to see if after all I've been through and all I've conquered, if I could finally pass and get a diploma." "Is it that important to you? Look around you. Look what you've done here in this town. You have so much to be proud of," she told me. "Why don't you think about that?" I knew that and I understood and appreciated what she was saying but school was something else, something I had to do for me, not the kids, not the parents, not the town, but for me.

After a good night's sleep, I was back to normal. The program was doing fine but time was running out on our five thousand dollar donation to pay the rent. We were now well into our ninth month and had only one month rent left and I knew we needed a miracle. I was sitting in the residential facility one evening and one of the female residents knocked on my office door and walked in. "Al, Congressman Stu McKinney is on the phone for you." Stu and I had become good friends. "Stu, how are you?" I said. "You sitting down, Al?" "Yeah, what's up?" "Operation S.P.E.A.R. was just funded for 8 million dollars. Congratulations," he said. I could have hit the ceiling, I was so happy. I thanked Stu for his help. We spoke a little longer and hung up. "I knew it," I told myself, "I knew this. It had to happen; we're doing good work here. We weren't asking for money to start something. We were asking for money to continue doing what we had been doing for so long and that, I'm sure, made it so much easier."

The first one I called was my mother who knew our situation and was very worried. She was very happy and very proud of her son and that's just the way I wanted her to feel. Knowing my mother, I'm sure she must have called the entire family; she was as excited as I was. An eight million dollar grant doesn't mean you get a check for eight million dollars. Number one, there are matching funds that you have to raise. Each year, your end of the matching funds gets higher. This was also an eight year grant so by the end of eight years you have matched the same amount or close to the same amount that they have given you which means that an eight million dollar grant is only four million from them and four million from you. I then called Stu, who worked so hard on this project. "Stu," I said, "when you come in tomorrow bring your name-plate. You have a job." I then called the Chairman of the Board. Next, I called a house meeting, a meeting of all the residents and told them the good news. When you talk to a group of kids, you always try to add some teaching in your speech. "Now that we have money to function, we're going to be bringing in more residents. That's why you people have to learn as much as you can, as fast as you can, so that you can help teach whoever is coming in. Unless we help one another and teach one another, this program can not work and it's your responsibility to help others, just as you were helped." We then put on the music and had a party.

A few weeks later, I opened my mailbox and found a letter from the Board of Education. I opened it expecting to read that I had failed. "Congratulations," it read. I had passed all my tests and the scores were listed. Math was my highest score. "Amazing," I thought. The truth is, I would have felt much better if I had passed because I knew the answers, not because I guessed. The diploma now was not a sign of accomplishment; it was just a piece of paper.

I had hired a married couple, Juan and his wife Lydia, to run the residential facility. I had known Juan from Daytop and we were very good friends. Juan was sent to Daytop from Puerto Rico on a court case he had. We became friends from the first day he arrived in Daytop. In fact, I was the one that taught him his first English word. That's right, the one you're thinking of now. Juan would direct the house and his wife was the assistant director. I was so glad to have them both with me, but what I didn't know was that Juan had a drinking problem. At first, things seemed fine but soon I started to see signs that things weren't going well at the house. Every time I called the facility, I was unable to reach the director or the assistant director and problems were popping up pretty often. One day, I called Juan to the office and gave him a verbal reprimand. I let him know I wasn't happy with his performance or his attitude. Juan walked out of the office crying. Less then ten minutes went by and his wife was knocking on my door. "Why did you make my husband cry?" she asked. In no uncertain terms, I let her have it also. "I don't have to explain anything I do to your husband to you. This is business, this is a therapeutic community and this is how we do things. If your husband chooses to cry over a verbal reprimand, that's his problem but don't you dare think for one minute that you can march in here and confront me for the way that I dealt with your husband."

In therapeutic communities, verbal reprimands are given out every-day and one learns to accept them and get the teachings from it. Juan and his wife didn't. They chose to start a hate campaign against me, telling friends from other programs that I didn't know what I was doing, that I don't hold good meetings and, in short, that I was a bad guy. These two people, who were both out of work and had contacted me for jobs, were taken in by me, given good jobs with good salaries and lived rent free in that four room cottage in the back of the facility, never appreciated any-thing. Knowing Juan as well as I do and understanding Lydia, I'm sure it was the alcohol talking and I hope by now they got it together.

Back in my office, things were going fine. Our proposal to the state of Connecticut and to the city of Norwalk was granted. We now had federal money, state money, and city money, and each, of course, had to have its own bank account. There were five bank accounts in all. Three, one each for the monies from the three government-funding agencies, another for the parents' organization, and one account for donations.

I started to hire more staff and expand a little. We started a pro-gram in the two middle schools in Norwalk and in two prisons. Other programs were contacting me for information on funding. We were the first program in Connecticut to be funded by the federal government and now we were helping others, just like we were helped. We're all here for the same reason and there must be a sharing of information. I turned those people over to Stu and Stu helped them all.

My mother kept coming up and would spend the time living with the females in the house. She kept telling me that the facility director and the assistant director are never present at morning meeting and that the residents themselves were running the meetings. Morning meeting is a very important part of the day. It starts with the reading of the S.P.E.A.R. philosophy:

"We were drawn inward in retreat from a hostile world to the loneliness of ourselves. Disturbed by what we saw through troubled eyes, we despaired. Ours is a desperate need to be nurtured by understanding, reassured by love and comforted by friendship until there is a rebirth of a responsible person

with dignity and pride, love and respect for ourselves and our fellow man. Reality becomes the center of our universe from which we no longer run. We learn that we can affect and direct our destiny as well as our place in society. We realize that each of us is a star taking his place among millions of others and that the world will be a little less bright without us, and above all else we realize that living is giving, sharing is caring and loving is to be loved."

Frank Descala, 1970

Along with that, morning meeting is used for announcements and for general discussion. It's geared for the residents to get off to a good start unless, of course, there are problems in the house at which time we may get right into that in no uncertain terms and they may not walk away with smiles on their faces. That's fine, too, because they are learning to control and to deal with their feelings, and they learn in time that even in a bad mood your responsibility comes first and you must deal with those feelings.

A few weeks later, I allowed some residents who had been around for a while and doing real good to go to a party. My director showed up at the party drunk. I could see that my married couple, the director and assistant director were not doing their jobs and causing big problems and it was time to deal with this situation in a way that I had hoped I never would have to. Juan was my friend for years and now I would have to fire him. It's never easy to fire anyone but it's even harder when it's a long-time friend. I knew that when I fired him his wife would leave also. If not, I would see that she left. I called him in and told him what he had done in the last eight months that were wrong and harmful to the program. Some of these things I had already spoken to him about. I explained that it was best if he left the program, best for all concerned. "You're firing me?" Juan asked me. I could see that he was getting a little crazy and a little loud and I didn't want any confrontations. "You can't fire me; there's a Board of Directors." "Yes, I can and yes, I did." "What about the Board of Directors?" he asked. "If you have any problems with my decision, feel free to contact the Board but, for now, pack your bags and get off my property." I had to end it as fast as I could to avoid problems and, to be honest, it was not easy for me to do. About three hours later, he and his wife left the grounds.

A house meeting was called to explain to the residents that the two of them were gone. I had learned a lot about these two before I made my decision and I laid it out for the kids. "They never were here for morning meeting, they would come in around eleven and stay a few hours and then leave, they would not be there for group encounters, and, in short, they weren't doing their jobs. Although we don't always do the right thing because we still have so much to learn about ourselves and about life itself, we still know right from wrong and there are things that these two taught you that were very meaningful. You know what those things are. I suggest that you use those things because neither of them would have harmed you by teaching you the wrong thing. So, in doing so, try to remember them in a good light. They are going through some problems of their own; let's hope they find some answers."

Soon I started to go out with a parent. This is a "no-no" in this type of environment. I was attracted to her but had never said anything out of the way. One night at a parents' meeting, she told me that she wanted to introduce me to her sister-in-law and I said, "Fine." "I'll bring her to next week's meeting," she said. "Great, I look forward to it," was my answer. The following week Faith, the parent, showed up alone at the meeting. After the meeting was over, I asked her where her sister-in-law was and she said, "Oh, she's going to meet us at the bar." "O.K. I'll follow you to the bar and will meet her." Needless to say, my hunch was right. There was no sister-in-law but Faith and I did have a few drinks and wound up at my place. This relationship lasted about two years without anyone knowing about it which was really hard in a small town like Norwalk, Connecticut. However, you can't hide in a small town and eventually it was common knowledge that Al and Faith were a couple and it really never caused any problems, except for me knowing that it was wrong; well, I felt like that at the beginning but after two years I was fine with it. Faith was a good woman, kind, considerate, warm, affectionate, clean, and the best cook I ever met. This woman I should have married!

I was feeling a little burnt out and decided to take a short vacation. I was talking on the phone to a friend of mine who lived in Miami Beach and ran a program there called Operation Re-entry. Steve and I had grown up together. We started using drugs together and were even once in the same cell on Rikers Island. "Come down," he said. "You'll love it here. You can lay up at the pool during the day while I work and at night we can go out and enjoy ourselves. I'll show you around," he said. "Sounds good to me. I'll call you before I come down."

A few days later, Faith and I were on a flight to Miami. She hated flying worse than I did when I first got on a plane and I kept hearing about it. Ten minutes into the flight, I was still hearing about it so I said, "Watch the propeller. If it stops turning, then we have a problem." "There is no propeller," she said. "Oh, no," I said. "Did it fall off already?" Finally, she smiled. "I like your smile," I said. "Think you can do more of it on this flight." "No!" I knew now it was time to activate plan B. "Stewardess, may I please have a drink for the lady?" Faith was a cheap date, one drink and she was ready for new heights. From then on, it was an enjoyable flight.

We landed in Miami and took a cab to the hotel on Collins Ave. and 96th St. What a beautiful place this was. We had a room overlooking the pool to our right and the beach right in front of us. We unpacked, took a shower and Faith was hungry. "O.K. Let's get dressed and get something to eat," I said. "No," she said. "They have room service." "Room service, what the hell is room service?" I had stayed in so many fleabag hotels in my life and now for the first time was in this big beautiful hotel with class and I didn't know things like this existed. We ordered by phone, and a few minutes later there was a knock at the door. "Room service!" I opened the door, expecting to be handed a few bags when, all of a sudden, in walks this guy with a table. He opens the table, covers it and says, "I'll be right back with your food." He walked out for 10 seconds and then pushed this steam table in with him and started to serve us. 'Damn, this is cool,' I thought. "I like this."

The phone rang. It was my friend Steve. We made arrangements to meet in a club by the name of The Forge later that night. Faith was too knocked out from the flight so I went myself. I walked in and looked around. "What a nice place," I thought. I had never been a drinker and I knew nothing about places like this. I found Steve and his friend Sam standing at the bar, right in front of the bandstand where live music was playing. I had met Sam in New York before they left for Miami. Both of them had gone through a program in California named Synanon. We had a great night, a few drinks, much conversation and many laughs.

When we were younger, Steve and I were partners. We were together everyday. Back in those days, we were finding some way to come up with money to get high and we laughed at some of the things we did, wondering how we ever got away with so much. Now, the conversations were different. Now, when we talked, we look at it as if it were stupid. What stupid things we did or how stupid we were to think we could pull that one off. That is exactly how ex-addicts are supposed to be thinking and talking because now, of course, we were above all that. We didn't loose our sensitivity to others. We know there are people out there doing what we did, doing the stupid things we did and we understand fully that it's a way of life with them and, until they get some help and change themselves, that will remain a way of life for them. For us, it had changed and we were glad that it had. I rented a car, and Faith and I managed to see Steve and Sam almost every day, along with my friend Wally, who was working for a program in Ft. Lauderdale. We were having such a great time, lying out at the pool during the day, going out at night and seeing some of the beautiful sights that Miami has to offer. I was falling in love with Miami. We stayed ten days and I hated to leave but I had responsibilities that I had to get back to.

When I arrived home, I got in contact with Daytop and one day I drove down to Staten Island to meet with the director. "Billy," I said, "I want graduation status. I think I proved over the years that I maintain the teachings of Daytop, the values, the morals and the philosophy. I'm also a person that Daytop should be proud to have as a graduate." "I agree with you," he said. "It's not a problem. Al, give me a few days and I'll send you a diploma." "Not good enough, Billy. I want a graduation ceremony like any other resident going through the program." A few weeks later my girlfriend and I drove down to Staten Island for my graduation. I was introduced, given my diploma and I gave a short speech. In it I said, "No matter where I travel and no matter how many programs I get involved with, my heart will always be in Daytop. Daytop saved my life and I realize that I must carry the philosophy and the values of Daytop with me forever, and I will."

In 1973, I was nominated for Man of the Year in Norwalk. The contest was a nationwide event. First you win your city, then your state, and then the nationals. No, I didn't even come close to that. I came in second to my friend Larry who was a deserving winner in Norwalk. Nevertheless, it was a good feeling knowing that people in your town appreciate what you're doing and recognize the hard work you have put in. I thank the Nights of Columbus for that honor.

Back at the facility, I held a staff meeting to talk about kids ready to graduate from our program. There were, I think, eight kids that were ready so I went to the parents' organization and explained that these graduations are usually done in the facility but I wanted something better for my kids. I wanted our graduation to be done in a catering hall. The parents loved the idea. We rented a hall and sent out invitations to parents, friends and politicians. My mother, of course, was there with about 20 members of my family. It was a huge success. The philosophy was read and I took the podium, thanking everyone for sharing this evening with us. After talking about the progress of the program, I then called each kid, one at a time, talking a little about each of them and poking a little fun at them for the way they came into the program. One by one, they came up and got their diplomas and each of them expressed their appreciation for the help they had gotten. After I finished graduating all of them, I said, "There is another graduate I'd like to introduce to you. This woman has fought drug abuse in her own home with two sons that used drugs for a total of 25 years, serving 17 years in prison. Neither of her sons use today. One died of an overdose, and the other went through a program. Ladies and gentleman, I'd like to honor this lady tonight. Please greet my mother."

My mother was crying and came to the podium to a standing ovation. The president of the parents' organization handed her a beautiful bouquet of flowers. She went on to give a brief speech about how proud she was of me and then sat down. Then I heard, "Wait, wait, I'm coming to now," (she was over-whelmed) and she returned to the podium. "Let me tell you what my son did for me last night," she said. "When I arrived here last night, I realized I had forgotten the belt to this dress and I was so upset. Allan recognized this and asked what was wrong. I told him about the belt and he said, 'Don't worry, mom, I'll go to your house and get it for you.' My son drove all the way from Connecticut to Brooklyn to get my belt." I got a big hand and when she sat down, I said, "Don't worry, mom, you'll get a bill for the gas." She went through so much in her day, this was the least I could do.

One day I took in a female whose mother was a raving lunatic, only I didn't know it at the time. The mother got to hate the program. She never once came to a parents' group, never once spoke to a staff member to learn about the program, never once visited the program but she hated anything to do with operation S.P.E.A.R. I can only imagine that she felt inadequate as a parent and knowing S.P.E.A.R. was doing what she couldn't, must have destroyed her. She started to contact my Board of Directors making up lies about me, telling them untruths about me. When I went to a Board meeting, I found myself defending the work I had been doing. Almost every meeting for the next two years was the same. She then started to take in kids that had left the program. "Splitees" we call them. She, at one time, had about ten kids living in her house and word was they were all using drugs, including her. My psychiatric consultant suggested I ask the girl to leave the program in the hopes that the mother would let up and stop this campaign she had against me. I could not do that. I could not sacrifice this young girl the way I was sacrificed in school. I was saving lives and, if her daughter went back to drugs, her future would be very dim. I thought about it, I wrestled with the idea, but I could not bring myself to do that. Finally, the mother contacted the state of Connecticut who sent a representative down to investigate the program. She spent the entire day at the residential facility. I had left the grounds and let the state do whatever they had to. The report from the state was that there are no irregularities and that the program was a good, sound program and running smooth, but there were some problems.

There were other problems in the form of a black-run daycare center that was trying to take over my program and war started between us. They tried one day to plant staff in my facility. Once they asked me to do a speaking engagement at their facility. When I got there, they said that I have two minutes to talk. I said, "How do you talk about a program in two minutes?" They said, "That's what you have." I said, "Fine." I got up and said, "I'm sorry but I was told I only have two minutes to speak. That's not very much time to talk about a life-saving organization, so the best I can do is invite you all to the facility to see and to learn for yourselves just what we are doing. Please be my guest on any Saturday night." Then I left. The next thing I heard was that I was talking down to them because they were black.

A guy that I knew belonged to their organization came to me for a job. "Do you have any experience?" I asked him. "No, why do I need experience?" he asked. I explained, "We are in the business of saving lives and when you're dealing with people's lives, you better well know what you're doing." "If you don't give me a job," he said, "I'm going to put an article in the paper saying you won't hire black people." "Go ahead," I said, "knock yourself out." A day before that, I had driven with a black councilwoman from Norwalk to the other end of the state to interview her daughter who was in jail. The girl didn't want to come to the program. That same day that the guy came for the job, this councilwoman called me up screaming that we don't take black kids. "I'm going to the papers," she said. "I'm putting an article in there saying that you don't take black kids." Reality was we took all kids. "Go ahead, my dear," I said, "because I'll be writing a counter article explaining how I just drove you to the other end of the state to interview your daughter in the hopes of getting her into the program. I think I'll add that you didn't even offer the gas money that the program paid for. Where is your head?" I said. "How easily we forget the people that try to help us," I added. Those two incidents were designed by that daycare center director.

One day the Probation Department set up a meeting with me and the head of that daycare center. I brought a black staff member who was a graduate of the Renaissance project with me. The Director walked in with another guy and they jumped all over my staff member. "How can you work for this white guy?" they asked. Just like that, I couldn't believe my ears. My staff member looked at them and said, "This white guy, as you call him, saved my life in Renaissance and there aren't too many people that know this business as well as he does. He's my boss and my friend and that's just the way it's going to stay."

Needless to say, the meeting became a war. They were yelling and screaming and I wasn't backing down but I never raised my voice, which got them madder. Then they demanded that I expand to their facility. Sure, what they wanted was to be able to say they now have a drug program and, as soon as they learned a little, I'd be out the door. They wouldn't learn enough because it takes years and they wouldn't get close enough to me to learn anything but that wasn't their concern. They just wanted funding to put more money on the table. The kids didn't mean a thing to them, lives didn't mean a thing to them, families didn't mean a thing to them, just money. I had learned through one of my residents who once was a member of their program that they teach kids how to cheat on their income tax and to hate whites. I never knew if that was right but, seeing their actions, I assumed it was. I had seen people like this so many times before. Jails are loaded with people who think they are above everyone and everything. This meeting went on like this for about an hour. "Are you going to expand to my facility?" he asked. "No,"

I said. "I'm not in any position to expand right now." "Then let me say for the record, Al. I'm going to do everything in my power to destroy your program." I turned to the probation officer and said, "Yes, yes, put that on the record," and I walked out.

This went on and on for the better part of two years. I was winning every battle but I was losing the war. The problem was that I was getting burnt out. I didn't come to Norwalk for war. I came there to start and run a drug rehabilitation center, to save lives, to help kids and their families, but not for war. I soon started to think about leaving. I came to Norwalk and started a program from scratch. I started with five thousand dollars and a burnt out office and built this great program. My Board of Directors, who claimed I'd run the program while they'd raise the money, never raised one cent. I did it all. I had built the finest program in Connecticut. I had a daycare center with about 50 kids, a residential center with about 55 kids, a school program, a jail program, a parents' organization, a siblings group, and I helped so many in the process. Now, it was time for me to move on. I had given Norwalk four years of hard work and dedication and, in doing so, saved many lives, but Norwalk wasn't coming to my aid. My Board of Directors was questioning me like I was wrong. I was hearing stories about my being drunk at a party that I wasn't even at and I don't even drink more than one or two at a time. I was hearing rumors about my smoking marijuana. Not only that, but some people were telling my girlfriend that I was cheating on her. They told her I tell everyone about the sex we have and so much that I can't remember all, so I decided to call it quits, to throw my hands up and say to hell with all of them. I knew that if I left, they would soon see what they had lost and, after licking my wounds, I'd be fine again and help others in another place.

I called my friend in Florida and soon flew down for an interview, which he had set up, as a facility director with a program in Miami. I was hired, came back to Norwalk and packed up my belongings and moved on. As I was driving down Interstate 95, it was bittersweet. I felt a sense of pride and a sense of sadness. I thought about the entire picture, going back to the days when I first met with the Board of Director, my first days in the health department, moving into the new day care facility, that burnt out office, getting my first kid, building a population, a few at a time, procuring the residential facility, getting the funding necessary to maintain these facilities, helping the parents and the community in general. I thought about the radio show, the speaking engagements I did. I thought about people that helped me, the people who gave so much to the program. I thought about the parents' group and the friends of the program, the few siblings we had worked with. I thought for hours and hours and that gave me a sense of accomplishment.

I was sad also and tears were rolling down my cheeks as I drove down the highway. I felt like I had lost all I had built and everything I had worked so hard for. I started to think of the people who caused me problems, the black daycare center director, the crazy parent, the splitees that lived with her, and the counsel-woman. I dedicated myself for all those years and now all I had to show for it was a history. A good history but, still, a history. I was sad, my girlfriend was sad, the parents' group was sad, and I knew the kids were sad; some were crying when I announced that I was leaving. Friends that I met and made over the years were sad, I'm sure, but I had to move on. I had to do what I had to do for me and the first two things I had to do was move on and put this all behind me.

In Florida, I got an apartment in my friend's building in North Miami. Also living in the building were two friends from Daytop who were now married. It was like old home week. I was in love with Miami. I moved into my apartment on July 4th, 1974. Yes, Independence Day. I let an elderly couple stay a few extra days that they asked me for. The elderly couple had lived there before I moved in. I had the opportunity to meet these nice people who were moving into a retirement home. The woman told me, "I cleaned the entire place for you, including the refrigerator and stove. You could move right in." My God, I thought, what a nice couple and so thoughtful also. The apartment was a large one bedroom on the second floor overlooking the pool. It was a very nice place. I started to learn my way around finding my favorite stores, restaurants and barbershop. Soon I was feeling at home. Still licking my wounds, but loving Miami. I started going to see all the attractions, the Miami Sea Aquarium, Fairchild Tropical Gardens, Parrot Jungle, Monkey Jungle and the Metro Zoo. I was having a great time but still with a heavy heart, but the most important thing was that I was slowly putting this entire thing behind me.

I remember my first New Year's Eve in Miami. We had a party at the pool and I loved it. "New Year's Eve at the pool in shorts." I thought, "How great is that? People up north can't even imagine this." All my New

Year's Eve's before were with top coats on and the wind blowing in my face, and now I'm sitting at a pool with a short sleeve shirt. "I like this," I said to my friend Wally. "This is great!"

My first day on the new job, when I walked into the facility, I was dumbfounded. The building needed a paint job, windows were broken, light fixtures were hanging from the ceilings, and there was only one air conditioner and that was in the director's office. "Is this the way they house kids?" I thought. This is the way most of these kids lived while using drugs and we're supposed to show them a better way and this is not it. I am a firm believer that if you treat a man as he is, he will stay as he is, but if you treat him for what he should be, then he will become what he should be and this was no way to do it. My God, think about it, housing kids in Florida where the humidity gets higher than the temperature without air conditioning is cruel and especially during mosquito season. Are these kids supposed to function as they should under these conditions? It would be very hard to find them at their full potential.

I also had a strange staff. We had a gay guy working in the facility, a nice guy who I liked and became very friendly with. One day a resident walked into my office and complained that the guy grabbed him and kissed him on the lips. I confronted the staff member and he said, "Oh, this is common in my country. That's how we greet people." "Was I supposed to believe that?" I thought. "Well, we're not in your country," I said. "This is America and in this country men don't kiss men on the lips unless they're gay, and in this situation only one of you is gay. This kid is having a problem with this and you put him in that position and that's not right, and I plan on doing something about it." I went to the Executive Director about this and nothing was done; nothing was said. I also suspected that a female staff member was having sex with a resident. Nothing was done about that either. I tried like hell to get the facility fixed up but never had the right equipment or resources to do anything. I continued on running my facility as best I could with what I had. It was very frustrating for me trying to do what I believe to be right and finding walls up wherever I turned.

One day my mother called asking if she could stay with me for a few weeks. "Sure, mom, come on down; you'll love Miami." I was single, and my apartment was pretty active but sometimes you have to put things on the shelf to please your mother. About two weeks later, I picked her up at the airport. We met at the carousel. I gave her a big hug and kiss and was glad to see her. The carousel started to turn and out came the suitcases. "That's one of my suitcases," she said. "O.K. I got it," I said. "That one also." "Got it, mom." "Wait, there's more," she said. I took four large suite cases off the carousel, loaded my car and on the trip home asked my mother, "How long are you planning on staying?" "Surprise," she said, "Aunt Bobbie and Uncle Sid got me an apartment across the street from them in Ft. Lauderdale. I'm moving in two weeks from today." "Great," I thought. I had missed my mother and I knew she missed me. She went on to say that she's close enough to see me and far enough away not to bother me. My mother realized I was still single and had an active sex life. I remember once, while still using drugs, I was making love to this woman on my couch and we both fell asleep naked. In the morning my mother woke me by tapping me on the shoulder. "Do you and your friend want breakfast?" she asked very softly, not to wake the girl. "Yeah, ma, go, go."

My mother never dated after my father died, never once and she was in her thirties, and a very beautiful woman, I may add. She used to cry my father's name while sleeping; I remember well, it always affected me. She was a very devoted woman to my father. My brother and I would always try to get her to go out but she kept saying, "I'll see." Just like my brother had said when I tried to get him to go to Daytop with me. "I'll see." My uncles, who were well-to-do businessmen, tried to introduce her to men. She never once met anybody.

After about six months down in Miami and still in contact with Faith from Connecticut, she called one night. "I got bad news for you," she said. "Operation S.P.E.A.R. is closing its doors." "What?" "Why? "What happened?" I asked. "I don't have too many of the particulars," she said, "but I'm sending down pictures of the kids getting on a bus to go to other programs." Stu, my administrative assistant, took the helm when I had left and I knew that was a bad decision. Although Stu knew the workings of the program, he had no idea how to run it. He was an administrative wiz but not a therapist and that's what you have to be to run a good program. Remember, it's a therapeutic community, not an administrative community. Can Stu be a therapist for kids, no, and he's supposed to be the father figure. Did Stu know when mistakes were made by staff, other than with their paperwork? No. Stu, according to my girlfriend, had no idea what was going on. And the shame was it cost the best program in Connecticut to close.

The parents' group would not follow his lead and that got him crazy to a point that he was talking bad about me. When I heard that, I called to confront him and he refused to get on the phone so I talked to his wife until I was sure he didn't have the nerve to be confronted. Then I just sent him a message through his wife, saying that I would like him to call me back; he never did. I didn't expect he would. My friends just kept telling me to wash my hands of the whole thing. It was not easy because I had worked so hard to build that program but the reality was, it wasn't mine any more and I decided my friends were right.

I continued working for the program in Miami and day after day, week after week, I went to work trying to make things better. One day, a resident who was on our procurement team came to me and said that he thinks he's getting 160 gallons of paint from this paint company. "Great," I said. "Now we can paint the house." The Executive Director got word of this and called me on the phone, yelling at me. "Are you crazy? You're going to paint a house that is condemned? When the paint comes in, you get it to me," she said. The truth is, I had no idea the building was a condemned building. I knew it should have been, but had no idea it was. There was a lack of communication that should never have been. Therapeutic communities revolve around communication and the staff has to lead the way. That's why I was so unsuccessful in getting anything fixed, that's why I was so unsuccessful in getting air conditioners, new light fixtures, windows and everything else that was needed. Now, after about a year, they decide to tell me that the building has been condemned and they call me stupid. It wasn't easy working there. The higher-ups made it tough with their decisions and the conditions made it tough to function, but I continued on. I did decide to leave but not until I found another job.

One day in conversation with my friends, I heard about a program run by the federal government to legitimize ex-addicts involved with programs. They would give you credits for the time you served in prison, credits for your going through a program and credits for your work in these programs after you graduated from a program. They took 90 ex-addicts from across the country that had put the most time into working in therapeutic communities and put them in an all-girls college, while the girls were away for Christmas vacation, to give them A.A. degrees hoping they would go on and get their B.A.'s and more. The school was Marjorie Webster Jr. College in Washington, D.C. Because of the long service to the field of drug rehabilitation, I was one of the people picked to go for the course.

Here I was in college and I joked with myself. I was a 36-year-old with a GED that I had to guess the answers to pass and now I'm a freshman in college. This is crazy but the government wanted me to have the A.A. degree, so I went for it. I unpacked my things after being given a room, met the other people involved and got ready for my start of college. Orientation started and we found out where to be at what times. To my amazement, these degrees were handed to us. They gave us textbooks and we'd bring them to class, the teacher would teach and then give us a test to be taken back to our rooms and finished there. Well, all the answers were in the back of the book. Here you had 90 ex-addicts, most of whom never spent much time in school, like myself, in college, with the answers in back of the textbooks.

I remember calling my mother to find out how she was and she asked how I was doing and I said, "Well, so far I've gotten an 'A' on every test." "That's wonderful," she said and I started to laugh. "Ma, relax. The answers are in the back of the book. Everyone here must have an A average." We both know my education is null and void and I just have to live with it. I just could not mislead her.

A meeting was held in the auditorium one day for the heads of the funding agency to address the student body. What they were talking about was paperwork. Let me explain that most addicts follow the same path as I did. Out of school at a young age and with very little education was just about everyone's story that was there. It was explained to us that programs will be evaluated on paper from the reports we send them. The speaker was going on and on about this need for paper work, how important it is, how it tells them what is happening in your program. Soon they turned it over for questions and answers.

After some people asked some questions, I raised my hand to give a statement. I explained to them that they are asking the wrong people for paperwork. Most of us, I explained, were out of school since we were children. Can we run affective programs? Yes, we can. We run the best in the country. In my eyes, there is none better than the therapeutic communities run by ex-addicts, but you will never know that if you're evaluating us on paper. I appreciate the A.A. degree you are giving me but, in reality, it doesn't make me any smarter than the day I walked through your doors. How can uneducated people, not stupid, but uneducated people who are not equipped for paperwork, be able to communicate just how effective his or her program is if they are not adapted to paperwork? You need hands-on evaluators. If you're evaluating programs run by ex-addicts, you need ex-addicts to evaluate these programs, and they have got to do it by visiting the programs, spending time there, seeing what's going on, talking to the residents, sitting in on group encounters and seminars and talking to the staff. They should be checking to see if the facility is clean. Bathrooms, bedrooms, kitchen area and, in general, the entire facility should be spotless. If these things check out, then you have evaluated a good program. Paperwork is needed, I agree, but not to a point that it evaluates a program, not to a point that funding depends on it. We are a different breed. We're doing things that the so-called professional was unable to do; now you're asking for that professional to evaluate us. You can't imagine how many professionals have come into my program and said, "This is wonderful. You're getting kids off heroin without substituting another drug. I never could do that." Now you want these people to evaluate us, the same people who said we were doing what they can't. I would hope, sir, that you reconsider your proposal. With this, I sat down and got a round of applause from my fellow students.

Did it help us any? I don't really know. I never did see any extra paperwork coming our way but the government moves slowly. To give you an idea how slow they move, they were telling us that in about 10 years from then marijuana would be decriminalized, and about 10 years later, two states did decriminalize it.

Knowing my degree was the same as my GED was once again not the greatest feeling in the world but I did enjoy Washington. I particularly liked Georgetown. I found that to be a very nice town. I also went to a Washington Bullets game when they beat up on my New York Knicks. That wasn't too much fun because the guy I was with was a Bullet fan. You could imagine the ride home. It reminded me of my brother and myself during the World Series when the Yankees would beat my Dodgers year after year. I couldn't wait till we got back to the campus. Let me say to all the New York Knicks fans that I am now a very loyal Miami Heat fan. Sorry about that, guys. After three weeks, I was given my diploma and headed back to Miami.

Now I was back at this program in this rundown building doing what I could to help these kids. One day the program director came to my facility and, without discussing anything with me and not showing me the proper respect, sat with my staff and made changes that were unbelievable. I was listening in amazement. What are these people thinking about? How do they run a program? At that point, I just let it out. "How dare you come into my facility and change things when you have no idea what's going on here? You haven't spoken to me and I know you haven't spoken to my staff and you come into my facility and make changes on a guess, on a hope and a pray. Thats not the way to run a program. You're dealing with lives here, and you have to see the entire picture before making decisions. You should at least have spoken to me first.

The next day I was called to the office and fired, which I knew was going to happen and I felt a sense of relief. I was glad to get out of there. I should have quit a long time before that but I felt a responsibility to the kids. Now, they weren't my responsibility any more. Now, let someone else go through the torture of trying to help kids in an inept facility where the staff hates to leave the office and be down on the floor with the kids because the only air conditioner we had was in the office. You can't run a program from your ivory tower. You have to be down there with the kids, watching, talking and teaching. This is not a game. You're dealing with people's lives, and if you want kids to change their ways, you have to be there to guide them. They're not going to change on their own. They are comfortable the way they are. It's easier for them this way; change is hard. They had lived like this for so many years. Can you change on your own? I think not. Even if they stopped using drugs, what about the problems that led them to use in the first place? The inadequacies, the fears, the hang-ups, the way of thinking, the lack of morals, values and convictions. Those are the things that need to be addressed and changed to get people to start feeling good about themselves. So, even if a kid stops using drugs, he or she still has to face the world not feeling good about himself or herself. That's not an easy task and most will fail at whatever they do. It's sad but that's the reality.

I felt sorry for the residents of the program. Some were trying real hard and don't misunderstand this, some were getting what they came to get. Some were giving it their all and using the tools of the program in a positive way but there was extra added stress that they didn't need and shouldn't have had. Pressure that was unwarranted, an uncomfortable feeling when you're feeling stress from your work assignment, from your department head, from the staff at times and, at the same time, you're feeling dirty and sweaty and stinky all day. Not a good feeling, not at all. We do our best to show residents of the program a better way, a cleaner way, a safer way and a healthier way. We try to get those that came from the slums, out of the slums and here they were living in a commended building. Where's the teaching in that?

I decided to take a few weeks off. I relaxed by the pool and at the beach, and spent time working on and getting new plants. I must have had about twenty-five plants in my house and on my catwalk in front of my apartment. I even had this coconut palm that I found. When I found it, there were two little leaves coming out of a coconut and I planted it in a pot in front of my window on the catwalk. In two years, it had reached the floor above me so I gave it to the building. The workmen planted it at the pool in front of my apartment and soon it reached the third floor from ground level. It grew so fast once it was taken out of a pot and placed in the ground. It was beautiful.

Soon, it was time to get back to work. I took a job with my friend as a facility director in his program in Miami Beach. That was a very well-run program in a beautiful facility. It was a day care program with about fifty kids, one block away from the beach on Collins Ave. I enjoyed working there. My friend and I lived in the same building and most days would travel to and from work together. I also was living in Miami and I loved life here. Miami, to me, was beautiful and I loved not having to drive in snow. I stayed at this program for a while longer, but was feeling tired of programs. The year was 1977. I was thirty-seven years old and I had been involved with drugs on one level or another for twenty-five years, dating back to when I first saw my brother and his friends getting high. I had used for 9 years, spent over five years in prison, and was involved with rehabilitation programs for eleven years and by now I was feeling burnt out, tired. I just felt like I had to get away, to go on my own and make a life for myself but where can I go? What can I do? My education was almost nothing. Everything I learned, I learned on my own and through programs, but how many seminars can you do, how many speaking engagements can you give, how many group encounter sessions and marathon sessions can you attend?

I thought about it for a long time, and at the same time was speaking to people in the business world and everyone said almost the same thing. Everyone pointed out one thing to me. "Al, you're a salesman; that's what you do. You sell a philosophy, a way of life; you're a natural born salesman." I never thought of it that way. I had thought of my career as a teacher, more than as a salesman, but these were very smart businessmen I was talking to who knew the business world much better than I did. This I had to think about. I stayed at my job but continued to think. Can I make it as a salesman? Can I be a good salesman? The field I was in gave me everything. It gave me life, it gave me respect, it gave me status, it gave me a reason and, in short, it gave me everything I had, and after eleven years could I, should I, try something else?

After a few months of thinking and realizing I could always return to this field if I decided to, I took a job as a salesman with a carpet company. I was doing rather good but soon found out from some old-time salesman that this wasn't the most honest business to be in, and I could not do what they expected me to do. Understand, not everyone does this, but some do. "Tack on an extra ½ yard to each sale," they said. "An extra ½ yard," I said. "That's peanuts. Why would I want to rob people for an extra ½ yard?" Then I was told, "Sell an extra ½ yard to each customer and at the end of the year, if you sold 500 jobs, you wind up with 250 extra yards sold. Sell one type of padding and give a less expensive one." No, this wasn't for me. I just couldn't bring myself to do anything like that. I am 100% honest and knew I had to stay that way. At the same time, I had a store manager pressing me to do this but I could not challenge my values and I would not change my morals. I soon decided to give that up but at the same time was glad to be away from rehabilitation programs. I soon was running short on money and had to get something soon so until I found out what I wanted to do, I took a job driving for a courier company, Sunshine State Messenger Service. Right off the bat, I got friendly with the dispatchers and was doing rather well. After a while, I was doing so good that I gave up thinking about other things. I always liked driving. Remember, I had five cars before I had a license. Driving, for some reason, relaxes me.

I started to date this very nice woman from Miami and things were going real well. I was making good money, had a nice girlfriend, and continued to enjoy Florida. A nice bunch of people moved into my building and, although they were all married and I was single, we all used to go out together. It was also great because each night all the guys would end up in my apartment and we were all sports fans who loved the Miami Dolphins. Every Sunday we would have a cookout at the pool, weather permitting. One of the wives would make the cole slaw, another, the potato salad, another, the macaroni salad and there was one guy who worked at a catering business who would bring the chicken and ribs. It was a pool party almost every Sunday and after we ate, someone would bring a small T.V. to the pool area and the football game would be put on. I was living a great life. I was happy, my mother was happy and life seemed great.

In 1982, I had twin daughters by this woman I had been dating for a while. Today, they are grown women with children of their own. I have three grandchildren. They all live in Georgia now. They are good kids and the grandchildren are beautiful and smart. My children know nothing about my past as there was never a need to tell them. I guess this book says it all.

In 1986, I met a beautiful young lady from Venezuela and married her. Things were going well for us until I found out that her two sons, who I met only a few times before we got married, were using drugs. Now the shoe was on the other foot. It's true what they say, what goes around comes around. Now I had two sons that were drug addicts, but these kids were worse than I was in the fact that almost every time they walked into my house, they stole something. The older one couldn't be trusted out of your sight for one second. The younger one I don't think ever took anything. At least when I was using, I never once stole anything from any relatives' house or even from a friend's house, for that matter. I never even thought about it; it never even entered my mind. The difference between us is called class, it's called loyalty, it's called family. The younger one was a good kid that was swayed by his older brother much like I was.

This created problems between my wife and me. We argued a lot over her sons. Whatever they did was O.K. with her. That was for a long time the only arguments we ever had, all about her children, until later on in years we had argued so much about them that we started to argue about anything. She started to lie to me about them and she started to cover up things they had done. Things got so bad that I decided we could no longer stay married and I suggested a divorce which came soon after. We were together for 12 years, married for 10.

Shortly after my marriage, my mother got real sick and could not manage on her own so she moved in with my wife and me. My wife, being the caring person that she was at the time, took great care of my mother. She cooked for her, bathed her, did her laundry, cut her fingernails and toe nails and would sit with my mother for hours talking to her. For this, Sony will always be my friend. We divorced in 1995. My mother passed away in 1989 at the age of eighty-one. I still, and will always, miss her.

I also found that I love to travel. When I was married, we visited my wife's country of Venezuela five times. I also have been to the Dominican Republic, Mexico, Toronto, Nicaragua, and Panama one time each, but the country I love the best is Costa Rica. I have been to Costa Rica five times and just loved every minute of each trip. I love the country and I find its people to be the nicest, cleanest and most honest of any country I have ever been to. I have very dear friends living there, Jeanette and Bernardo, two beautiful people who I visit each time I'm there. Some day I would love to build a house high on a mountain top in that country.

After 12 years as a courier with Sunshine, I got into the airfreight business and still, to this day, am doing the same work. Today I am 68 years old with some health problems but nothing life-threatening. I still live in Miami. I have a very nice place in the Fontainebleau area about ten minutes west of Miami International Airport. Miami International is the port of entry to South and Central America and if you're doing air freight this is where you want to live. I deal mostly with aircraft parts shipping all over the country and around the world. One thing for sure, there will always be a need for someone to move aircraft parts. Planes are very well-maintained and parts are changed all the time. The area, Fontainebleau, is a very nice, clean and safe area and I've been living in this area since 1990.

Today I am a very happy person. I enjoy people, have many friends and like my work. I am reunited with family that I love, but, most of all, Allan loves Allan and that's the feeling that was so hard to get. That, to me, is the most important feeling in the world. You can't love others till you love yourself and I'm ready to love the world. I realize I have been through a lot since I was a young child, starting with the school system that misunderstood my condition, my mother that wasn't strong enough to show me the right way, my brother who raised me wrong, the probation department and the social workers that let me slide by. I hold no ill feeling towards anyone. Today, thanks to a lot of other people like the Daytop family, I am my own man and I will continue to stay that way. It has been over forty-two years since I left prison on August 16, 1966 and I am very proud of that. During my years as an addict, I had done a lot of wrong and hurt a lot of people for which I am sorry but, over the last forty-two years, I have tried to make up for that and I hope in God's eyes I have.

I guess you can say this completes my book, but my story doesn't end here; life goes on. I once said that I would never look back. This book brought me back and trust me when I say it was not easy. There were so many times that I typed with tears in my eyes because I had been through so much in my life ever since I was a small child and unable to compete in school, when I felt stupid and fat, when I learned my father had died, and again when Abe told me my grandfather would never be sick again, when grandma passed away, when I was put away for the first time at thirteen years old, walking up those steps and hearing my mother crying in the courtroom. When I walked into a penitentiary for the first time looking down the cell block and walking into the small pale green cell that would be my home for the remainder of my stay there. Thinking of how my mother felt having her son put in jail. Recounting the beatings in the police stations and the violence of prison life. The times I spoke to and asked my brother to come with me to Daytop. Recalling the last time I saw him and then when I learned he had died.

All this has been very hard for me to write, but I did it for a number of reasons. First, to make parents and teachers more aware of the problems of ADD and ADHD and what it could lead to if not diagnosed and treated in the proper manner and as soon as possible. Parents have to be aware of their kids' every move, to look for signs of kids being distracted and not paying attention and, of course, being depressed. Parents and teachers alike should know the symptoms of ADD and ADHD:

- The child often fails to give close attention to details and makes careless mistakes in schoolwork, work or other activities.
- The child often has difficulty sustaining attention in tasks or play activities.

+ The child often doesn't seem to listen when spoken to directly.
+ The child does not follow through on instructions and fails to finish an assignment.
+ The child has difficulty organizing tasks and activities.
+ The child often avoids, dislikes or is reluctant to engage in tasks that require sustained mental effort.
+ The child often loses or misplaces things necessary for the task or activity.
+ The child is easily distracted by extraneous stimuli.
+ The child is forgetful and often forgets things that have to be done

(American Psychiatric Association)

It is so important for parents and teachers to look for these signs and to react to them right away. Today, thank God, there is medication for this problem and kids can go on to live a very productive life once treated.

Second, I want to make parents aware of the problems of drug abuse and/or any addiction and see that their child gets help as fast as they can. Parents have to become their child's best friend. They have to know their children, know everything about them, work with them, teach them, guide them and be there for them. I said so many times while giving speaking engagements that parents have to wear a number of hats. One is to be both the disciplinarian and a pal. That's not very hard if you love you child. Parents have to look for the signs of addiction as well. Children who withdraw from the family, become less involved. They start to hide things, change their normal hours or routines and don't communicate as much as they used to. In most cases, they will change friends and bring home kids that you have never seen before and become rebellious. They may start to spend more time in their rooms or away from the house. I often tell parents to check their child's room, go through their drawers and I'm told this is an invasion of their privacy. Remember, they are young and living in your house and you have every right to check the room they are staying in.

A word of advice to the single parents: It's so much easier when two parents, even though they are not living together, work as a team to give the best to their child. All too often, parents who split up compete to be Number One in the heart of the child. All too often, parents will talk bad about the ex-partner or overrule a decision that the other made hoping to be Number One. This is a terrible mistake and, in reality, works against you, rather than for you. There has to be teamwork and communication between both parties to raise this kid and mold him, her or them into well-rounded individuals capable of dealing with today's society.

If parents are living apart and the child has been bad to the point of being punished, then that child must be punished in both houses. I really prefer the expression "learning experience," rather than punishment. If the child is grounded in one house, then that child should be grounded in the other house as well. There must be communication between the two parents and please don't let your feelings towards the other one get in the way. Rise above your feelings; deal with your feelings. If you can't do that, then I must ask, who is more important, you or your child? God gave you the means to create a child but God never said he would raise this child for you, so while you're hoping and praying that the child grows up right with good morals, values and respect for themselves, you should be making sure that child grows up with this and more. That's your job!

For the single parent without a partner, it is never easy to be both mother and father. In fact, it's impossible but you could be both disciplinarian and pal. In all cases, parents must know the child, be a part of that child, share ideas with that child, do things with that child and, in short you must be that child. You should know more about the child than he or she knows about himself or herself. You have to sit with them while they do homework but never give them the answers, teach them how to find the answers, how to research a book or surf the net looking for the answers to questions that the school has given them. Get them involved with reading, open their minds, exercise their brains and always communicate with them. Let them see that they are a part of you, just like you are a part of them and if you're ever stuck for a decision, be rigid. If you're rigid, you're child is safe and if he or she thinks your decision was unjust, well then, I guess they are just going to have to deal with the feelings, something they have to learn to do anyway. If they are disappointed, fine. They have to learn that life is filled with disappointments and they had better start to learn how to deal with them now. If I may take a line from my dear uncle Bernie who always said, "I'd rather see them cry now, than have me cry later." I wish you all luck.

TEACHERS:

Sometimes we find a child that we think is incorrigible, bad or unstable, and destructive in class. We first have to realize that something brought that child to this point and that something is keeping that child there. It may only be a matter of finding what interests he or she has or giving him or her a little encouragement to find the answer to what causes this behavior. Giving that child a little extra may be the turning point, showing that you care. Helping that child along by giving a little extra really means only a few extra minutes, saying the right thing and giving of your knowledge. Your responsibility as a teacher is to teach all of the children. Don't sacrifice this child for the sake of the others. This behavior is an indication that the child needs help.

I once had a parent come into my office years ago who told me, "I have five children and treated them all the same. Yet, this one went bad." My answer to him was, " Maybe that's why. You treated them all the same and they are not all the same. They all have their own personalities, their own differences, and they all take things differently and deal with things differently. They are not a mass; they are individuals."

So, teachers, please, for those who need it, take that extra five minutes, give that encouragement, show that you care.

Third, to let drug abusers know there is help out there and you to can change your life and become a more productive person. Daytop saved my life but there are so many good programs out there and to not take advantage of this is foolish. Please, don't end up as my brother and so many of my friends did. We need you and you need us and together we can beat this. I used to work for a program that had a saying: "Drug addicts are beautiful people, when they're not using drugs." That's so true.

My target date to finish this book was August 16th, which is the 42nd anniversary of my release from prison and the day I returned to Daytop. It's also a bittersweet day because it was the last time I ever saw and spoke to my brother. I remember my brother so well, everything about him. The way he walked, the way he talked, and the way he smiled. I forgive my brother for the teachings he gave me. It was what he knew, the life he led. In his head, I'm sure, he thought it was right. My brother loved me very much. I always felt that and I hold no ill feelings. "Rest in peace, pal."

Today is Aug 16th ....I made my target date, but before I end this book, I'd like to talk about two very serious problems we have in this country today.

To change one of them, we must first change the meaning of the word "cool." That word has a negative overtone and should be changed to something positive and I think that we must start it with children. I think someone has to get into the schools and talk to kids of kindergarten, first grade and second grade age and speak about the word "Cool." If you walk into a classroom and ask kids who is "Cool," they will all raise their hands but ask them what "Cool" means and they have trouble answering that question. Great, the best place to start. I'll tell you what "Cool" is. "Cool" is a kid that listens to his parents. "Cool" is a kid that listens to his teachers. "Cool" is a kid doing his/her homework, studying and reading. "Cool" is helping your mommy around the house. "Cool" is playing nice with your friends. "Cool" is helping people, being kind to animals and so much more. We should give them pins to wear-"I'm Cool. I listen to my mommy." "I'm Cool. I do my homework," etc.

These young kids have to know at that age that it's better to do the right thing than the wrong thing. You want to stop drug abuse, then this is where you start. We must all admit that the value scale of this country has fallen so far from where it was when I was young, and something has to be done before it gets any worse and what better place to start then with the children, of course! They must grow up with good values and morals. They must grow up feeling good about themselves. They must have confidence and want to do the right thing and this is the job of every parent, every teacher and every person. Children are the ones that will run this country 30, 40 and 50 years from now. True, most of us won't be here then but what about your grandchildren and your great-grandchildren and so on down the line? What type of world do we want to leave behind? It gets worse every day so imagine how it will be if this trend continues.

The second problem is that of child abuse. Child abuse is the same as homicide, as far as I'm concerned. No matter at what age a child is abused, he or she will never forget that experience. That kid will live with those feelings for the rest of his or her life recounting over and over again the fear, the pain and the torment. This, to me, should be a capital crime and punishable the same way. I feel abusers of children should be locked up and have the key thrown away. In most cases, these poor kids are killed because the attacker is afraid to be identified by the children. I'm sure the thought is, well, if we threaten to throw the key away wouldn't they just kill the children? Well, they are doing that anyway and maybe the thought of going to prison and never getting out will stop some, maybe most. Are there any other suggestions? Throwing the key away would be a fitting end to a child abuser. To these abusers I say, if you don't commit the crime, you never have to worry about being identified. Something has got to be done. We are losing too many kids to these butchers of children.

Then there is verbal abuse by parents that has to be stopped also. These are your children; you brought them into this world. How can you destroy what you created? Verbal abuse is devastating to young children. It can destroy a child emotionally. It destroys their confidence, their self-assuredness; it takes away their energy, their integrity and their will and puts fear in their hearts. It takes the smile from their face and the gleam from their eyes. Children are the most beautiful thing we have on this earth and it's our responsibility to make them shine. If we do what we're supposed to do, then they will do what they're supposed to do and make you very proud of them. I don't think there are laws against verbal abuse but there should be; it's devastating. Problem is, there is no way to measure verbal abuse so you have to be your own judge and jury and know when to cut it off.

I always say, "Be good to the children because some day you will need them to be good to you."

I wrote this book to try to help people. With my education, I never thought I could write a book but my dear cousin, Donna Saltz of Staten Island, kept encouraging me to do so. "You can do it, Al," she would say. "You can do it." My cousin is a retired schoolteacher. I wish I had teachers like her who would have encouraged me, rather than sit me in the last row, last seat and tell me to be quiet. Thank you, Donna. You are so sweet.

I'd also like to thank my cousin Ian Saewitz, also of Staten Island, for the encouragement and the help he gave me with his computer skills and the design of the cover.

Thanks, Cuz.

To the Daytop family: Thank you so much; you saved my life.

Allan Rykoff